# One Hundred
# BIBLE STORIES
## Activity Book — Revised Edition

CONCORDIA PUBLISHING HOUSE • SAINT LOUIS

Edited by Rodney L. Rathmann

Scripture quotations are taken from the HOLY BIBLE, NEW INTERNATIONAL VERSION®. NIV®. Copyright
© 1973, 1978, 1984 by International Bible Society. Used by permission of Zondervan Publishing House. All rights reserved.

This publication may be available in braille, in large print, or on cassette tape for the visually impaired. Please allow 8 to 12 weeks for delivery. Write to Lutheran Blind Mission, 7550 Watson Rd., St. Louis, MO 63119-4409; call toll-free 1-888-215-2455; or visit the Web site: www.blindmission.org.

Manufactured in the United States of America

5    6    7    8    9    10                    15    14    13    12    11

# Contents

**Preface** 7

**The Old Testament** 9

*Primeval History (? to about 2000 B.C.)*
1. The Creation: The First to the Fourth Day. Genesis 1 9
2. The Creation: The Fifth to the Seventh Day. Genesis 1 10
3. Adam and Eve in Paradise. Genesis 2 12
4. The Fall into Sin. Genesis 3 13
5. The Promise of the Savior. Genesis 3 14
6. Cain and Abel. Genesis 4 15
7. From Adam to Noah. Genesis 5 16
8. The Flood. Genesis 6–9 17
9. The Tower of Babel. Genesis 11 18

*The Patriarchs (about 2000 to 1800 B.C.)*
10. The Call of Abram. Genesis 12 19
11. The Promise of Isaac. Genesis 18 20
12. Sodom and Gomorrah. Genesis 19 21
13. The Offering of Isaac. Genesis 22 22
14. Isaac and His Family. Genesis 27 23
15. Jacob's Stairway. Genesis 28 24
16. Jacob's Family. Genesis 37 25
17. Joseph and His Brothers. Genesis 37 26
18. Joseph Serves Pharaoh. Genesis 41 27
19. The Journeys of Joseph's Brothers. Genesis 42–43 28
20. Joseph Makes Himself Known to His Brothers. Genesis 44–45 29
21. Jacob and Joseph Are Reunited. Genesis 46–50 30

*Moses and the Giving of the Law (about 1500 B.C.)*
22. The Birth of Moses. Exodus 1–2 31
23. The Call of Moses. Exodus 3–4 33
24. The Passover. Exodus 11–12 34
25. The Departure from Egypt. Exodus 12–14 35
26. The Giving of the Law. Exodus 15–16; 19–20 36
27. The Golden Calf. Exodus 32; 34 37
28. The Bronze Snake. Numbers 13–14; 21 38

*The Occupation of Canaan (about 1460 B.C.)*
29. Israel Enters Canaan. Deuteronomy 34; Joshua 1–5 39
30. The Conquest of Canaan. Joshua 6–10 40

### *The Time of the Judges (about 1440 to 1100 B.C.)*

31. Gideon. Judges 6     41
32. Samson: Part 1. Judges 13–14     42
33. Samson: Part 2. Judges 15–16     43
34. Ruth. The Book of Ruth     44
35. The Boy Samuel. 1 Samuel 1–4     45

### *The Undivided Kingdom (about 1100 to 975 B.C.)*

36. King Saul. 1 Samuel 8–15     46
37. David Is Chosen. 1 Samuel 16–17     47
38. David and Goliath. 1 Samuel 17     48
39. David's Fall and Repentance. 2 Samuel 11–12     49
40. Absalom's Rebellion. 2 Samuel 14–18     50
41. Solomon and the Temple. 1 Kings 3–8     51

### *The Divided Kingdom (about 975 to 588 B.C.)*

42. The Prophet Elijah. 1 Kings 16–17     52
43. Elijah and the Prophets of Baal. 1 Kings 18     53
44. Naboth's Vineyard. 1 Kings 21     54
45. Elisha Sees Elijah Ascend. 2 Kings 2     55
46. Naaman and Elisha. 2 Kings 5     56
47. God Sends Jonah. Jonah 1–3     57
48. Jeremiah. Jeremiah 37–38     58
49. The Three Men in the Fiery Furnace. Daniel 3     59
50. Daniel in the Lions' Den. Daniel 6     61

## The New Testament

### *The Youth of Jesus (about 7 B.C. to A.D. 6)*

51. A Message for Zechariah. Luke 1     62
52. The Announcement to Mary. Luke 1; Matthew 1     63
53. The Birth of John the Baptist. Luke 1     64
54. The Birth of Jesus. Luke 2     65
55. Angels Announce the Savior's Birth. Luke 2     66
56. The Presentation of Jesus. Luke 2     67
57. The Magi from the East. Matthew 2     68
58. The Escape to Egypt. Matthew 2     69
59. The Boy Jesus at the Temple. Luke 2     70

### *The Public Ministry of Christ (about A.D. 29 to 33)*

60. The Baptism of Jesus. Matthew 3; Mark 1     71
61. The Temptation of Jesus. Matthew 4     72
62. Jesus Helps Peter Catch Fish. Luke 5     74
63. Jesus Changes Water to Wine. John 2     75
64. Jesus Calms the Storm. Mark 4     76

65. Jesus Heals a Man Who Was Paralyzed. Mark 2 — 77
66. A Widow's Son and Jairus' Daughter. Luke 7–8 — 78
67. Jesus Feeds More Than Five Thousand. John 6 — 79
68. Jesus Walks on the Water. Mark 6; Matthew 14 — 80
69. The Faith of a Canaanite Woman. Matthew 15 — 81
70. The Ten Lepers. Luke 17 — 82
71. Jesus Blesses the Children. Matthew 18–19 — 83
72. The Transfiguration. Matthew 17 — 84
73. Zacchaeus. Luke 19 — 85

### The Parables of the Savior (about A.D. 29 to 33)

74. The Lost Sheep and the Lost Coin. Luke 15 — 86
75. The Lost Son. Luke 15 — 87
76. The Foolish Rich Man. Luke 12 — 88
77. The Pharisee and the Tax Collector. Luke 18 — 89
78. The Good Samaritan. Luke 10 — 90

### The Passion and Death of Christ (about A.D. 33)

79. The Triumphal Entry. Matthew 21 — 91
80. The Anointing. Mark 14; John 12 — 92
81. The Last Judgment. Matthew 25 — 93
82. The Lord's Supper. Luke 22 — 95
83. Jesus in Gethsemane. Matthew 26; Luke 22 — 97
84. Jesus Is Betrayed and Arrested. Matthew 26; John 18 — 98
85. Jesus before the Sanhedrin. Matthew 26; John 18 — 99
86. Peter Disowns Jesus; Judas Dies. Matthew 26–27; Luke 22; John 18 — 100
87. Jesus before Pilate. Matthew 27; John 18 — 101
88. Jesus Is Crucified. Luke 23; John 19 — 103
89. Jesus Dies and Is Buried. Matthew 27; Luke 23; John 19 — 104

### The Glorified Christ (about A.D. 33)

90. The Resurrection of Christ. Matthew 28; Mark 16 — 105
91. The First Appearances of the Risen Lord. Matthew 28; John 20 — 106
92. Christ Appears to His Disciples. John 20; Matthew 28 — 107
93. The Ascension. Acts 1 — 109

### The Church of Christ (about A.D. 33 to 60)

94. The Holy Spirit Comes at Pentecost. Acts 2 — 110
95. The Crippled Beggar Is Healed. Acts 3 — 112
96. Stephen. Acts 6–8 — 113
97. Philip and the Ethiopian. Acts 8 — 114
98. Saul's Conversion. Acts 9 — 115
99. Peter Is Freed from Prison. Acts 12 — 117
100. Paul's Shipwreck. Acts 27–28 — 118

# *Preface*

For the past 50 years, *One Hundred Bible Stories* has introduced students and families to the truth and beauty of God's Word. Through the actual words of Holy Scripture and distinctive artwork, the history of God and His people comes alive on every page, drawing us into the story of God's grace revealed in Jesus Christ.

With the release of the new, revised edition of *One Hundred Bible Stories*, Concordia Publishing House is pleased to present the accompanying *One Hundred Bible Stories Activity Book*, a revision of *Working through God's Word*.

Already in its second revision, the popular *One Hundred Bible Stories Activity Book* is ideal for day school and Sunday school classrooms, for confirmation and midweek programs, for home schooling, and for family devotions. Each session poses engaging, relevant questions for classroom discussion and individual reflection. As with the previous edition, the activities have been written for persons ages 9 and above. Parents and teachers will welcome the ways that the two sections "Thinking about God's Word" and "Working with God's Word" draw students into the biblical story. An additional section, "Applying God's Word," has been added in this edition. In a world characterized by busy schedules and little time for reading and reflecting on God's Word, *One Hundred Bible Stories Activity Book* offers an interesting study and regular review of key narratives in Holy Scripture.

"Nuggets from the inexhaustible gold mine of the Scriptures." These words from the original Foreword still describe *One Hundred Bible Stories*. We pray that God will bless you as you read and study His Word, and that He will fulfill His purpose to use the Holy Scriptures to "make you wise for salvation through faith in Christ Jesus" (2 Timothy 3:15).

# 1  The Creation: The First to the Fourth Day
## (Genesis 1)

## Thinking about God's Word

1. What word tells who created the world? ____ _____

2. What is meant by "the beginning"? _____ _____

3. Who lived before the beginning? _____

4. Which words tell what happened every time God said, "Let there be"? _____

5. In what way does God continue to create the world today? _____ _____ _____ _____

6. How was it possible for God to create all things out of nothing? _____ _____ _____

7. In John 1:1–3 the Son of God is called "the Word." What connection is there between "the Word" and "God said"? _____ _____ _____ _____ _____

   Which persons of the Holy Trinity were active in the work of creation? _____ _____ _____

## Working with God's Word

*On the blank lines write on which day God created the following:*

1. Sun, moon, and stars ___

2. Day and night ___

3. Earth and planets ___

4. Land, trees, rivers and plants ___

5. Sky and water ___

*Fill in the blanks.*

1. In the beginning God _____ the heavens and the earth.

2. The earth was _____ and empty.

3. God separated the light from the _____.

4. God called the light _____.

5. The darkness God called _____.

6. God called the expanse _____.

7. God called the dry ground _____.

8. Each day consisted of evening and _____.

## Applying God's Word

1. Compare the world as God originally created it and the world in which we live. Note similarities and differences. _____ _____ _____ _____ _____

2. What do these first verses of Genesis 1 reveal to us about God? _____ _____ _____ _____

3. What does God's Word accomplish as we receive it in the Sacraments?_____ _____ _____ _____ _____

# 2 The Creation: The Fifth to the Seventh Day
### (Genesis 1)

## Thinking about God's Word

1. How can you tell that the Creator made a large number of living creatures in the beginning?

   _____
   _____
   _____
   _____

2. Which words show that God wanted the whole earth to be filled with living things? _____

   _____

3. Who is meant by "Us" and "Our" when God spoke about making people? _____

   _____
   _____

4. How many human beings did God make on the sixth day? _____ Which words show that God wanted them to have children who in time would live all over the world?

   _____
   _____

5. In what two ways did God say that people were to be rulers over the other creatures? _____

   _____
   _____

6. What was the chief difference between people and the other moving creatures? _____

   _____

7. Which words tell that there was not a mistake or a flaw in anything God had made? _____

   _____

8. How did God show on the seventh day that there was nothing more that He wanted to create? ___

   _____

9. Did God let the animals look out for themselves after He had created them? _____

   _____ How does He still preserve and govern them? _____

   _____

10. How does the picture try to show that there was peace and happiness among God's creatures?

    _____
    _____

11. Tell what God created on each day. Think of the wise plan God followed in what He made from day to day. _____

    _____
    _____
    _____
    _____
    _____
    _____
    _____
    _____
    _____
    _____

## Working with God's Word

*On the blank lines write on which day God created the following:*

1. Man ____
2. Cats ____
3. Turtles ____
4. Deer ____
5. Sharks ____
6. Cows ____
7. Whales ____
8. Worms ____
9. Chickens ____
10. Ants ____

*Fill in the blanks.*

1. God said, "Let birds fly above the _____ across the expanse of the sky."
2. God blessed them and said, "Be fruitful and _____ in number."
3. Birds and water animals were made on the _____ day.
4. God said, "Let Us make man in Our _____, in Our likeness."
5. So God created man in His own _____.
6. Male and _____ He created them.
7. God told them, "Fill the earth and _____ it."

10

8. On the sixth day God created animals and

   _____.

9. Everything that God made was very _____.

10. God _____ on the seventh day and made it
    holy.

## Applying God's Word

1. People are the most important visible creatures
   God made. Explain. _____

   _____

   _____

   _____

   _____

2. All Scripture points to God and His love for us in
   Christ Jesus. How does God's designation of the
   seventh day remind us of Jesus? See Matthew
   11:28. _____

   _____

   _____

   _____

   _____

3. How do the teachings of evolution compare with
   those of Genesis 1? _____

   _____

   _____

   _____

   _____

   _____

   _____

   _____

   _____

   _____

# 3 Adam and Eve in Paradise
## (Genesis 2)

## Thinking about God's Word

1. What was the difference between the way God made people and the way He made the other creatures? _____

2. How did God make woman? _____ Did she also have the image of God? _____

3. What place did God prepare as a home for the first married couple? _____

4. God revealed His glory and majesty in His great work of creation. How did He show His power? His wisdon? His goodness? _____
_____
_____
_____
_____

5. What is another name for Eden? _____

## Working with God's Word

*Fill in the blanks.*

1. God formed man from the _____ of the ground.

2. God breathed into man's nostrils the _____ of life.

3. Then man became a living _____.

4. God planted a garden in _____.

5. The tree of life stood in the _____ of the garden.

6. God put Adam into the Garden of _____ to work it.

7. God said, "It is not good for the man to be _____."

8. God said, "I will make a _____ suitable for him."

9. The woman was made out of one of Adam's _____.

10. The man said, "She shall be called _____, for she was taken out of man."

1. God formed woman of the dust of the ground.
   T   F

2. The Lord made every tree to bear good food.
   T   F

3. God put man into the garden to take care of it.
   T   F

4. There were two trees from which the man and woman should not eat.   T   F

5. Adam and Eve were holy.   T   F

## Applying God's Word

1. How does God describe the relationship He designed a man and a woman to enjoy in marriage? _____
_____

2. Why does God have a right to be adored by all creatures? _____
_____ Why has He a right to give them commandments? _____
_____
Why is it their duty to obey Him only? _____
_____

3. What actions of God, recorded in Genesis 2, evidence His love for people? _____
_____
_____
_____
_____
_____

# 4 The Fall into Sin
## (Genesis 3)

## Thinking about God's Word

1. How did God communicate with Adam and Eve?
_____

2. What special command had God given them?
_____
_____

3. How were they to show their obedience and love toward God? _____
_____
_____

4. Did they have the ability to fulfill God's command? _____

5. Tell how the first two people became disobedient.
_____
_____

6. Could Adam and Eve really hide from God?
_____

7. What came into the world as a result of Adam and Eve's disobedience? _____

8. Whose fault is it that we are sinners? _____
_____
_____
_____

9. Name four evils that have come into the world because of sin. _____
_____
_____
_____
_____

## Working with God's Word

*Answer the following questions.*

1. Who tempted the woman through the serpent?
_____

2. Who tempted the man? _____
_____

3. Who said they were not to eat of the tree of the knowledge of good and evil? _____

4. Who spoke the first lie in the world? _____
_____

5. How did the fruit look to the woman? _____
_____

6. Why did they try to hide from God? _____
_____

7. Where did they think they could hide? _____
_____

*Draw a line under the answer that makes each sentence correct.*

1. A serpent is a (servant—snake—eel).

2. This lesson is taken from the Bible in the Book of (Exodus—Numbers—Genesis).

3. Crafty means (hard—brave—sly—wise).

4. The serpent spoke first to the (man—woman—snake—tree).

5. The forbidden tree was the tree of (life—knowledge).

6. The devil tried to make the woman (curious—proud—afraid).

7. (God—Man and woman—Animals) brought sin into the world.

## Applying God's Word

1. What tactic did the devil successfully use to tempt Adam and Eve to sin? _____
_____
_____

2. Explain the meaning of the phrase "The eyes of both of them were opened." _____
_____
_____
_____
_____
_____

3. Why did Adam and Eve's relationship with God change when they sinned? _____
_____
_____
_____
_____

# 5 The Promise of the Savior

## (Genesis 3)

### Thinking about God's Word

1. What was the complete punishment the man and the woman deserved because of their sin? _____
_____

2. What sentence did God pronounce on the woman? _____
_____
_____

3. How was the serpent punished? _____
_____

4. Why did God clothe Adam and Eve after they had sinned? _____

5. Why did God not let them eat of the tree of life?
_____
_____

6. What is the most terrible consequence of sin? You will find the answer in Romans 6:23. _____

7. How did you become a sinner? _____
_____

8. What are some of the things Adam left behind when he lost Paradise? _____
_____

9. Look forward with Adam. Why could he still have hope in God's beautiful world? _____
_____

10. Look upward with Adam. What did he believe? What do you believe? _____
_____
_____
_____

### Working with God's Word

*Answer the questions with one word.*
1. Whom did the Lord God call? _____
2. How did Adam say he felt toward God? _____
3. Whom did the man blame for his sin? _____
4. Whom did the woman blame for her sin _____
5. Whom did the Lord God punish first? _____
6. Who would crush the head of the devil? _____
7. Who was to bring forth children in sorrow? _____
8. For whose sake was the ground cursed? _____

9. Who guarded the way to the tree of life?
_____

*Draw a line under the correct answer to each question.*

1. Whose fault was it that Adam sinned?
(devil's—Eve's—God's—Adam's)

2. Whose fault was it that Eve sinned?
(devil's—serpent's—God's—Eve's)

3. Who drove Adam and his wife from the garden?
(devil—cherubim—God—wild animals)

4. Why did Adam and his wife try to hide from God? (They were naked—They were as gods—They had sinned)

5. How did God punish Adam, his wife, and the serpent? (He killed them—He scolded them—He cursed them)

6. Who are sinners? (only heathen—all except Christians—only grown people—all people)

7. For whose sake did God curse the ground? (His sake—the woman's—Adam's—Satan's)

### Applying God's Word

1. In what ways do you experience the consequences of Adam's sin in your life? _____
_____
_____
_____

2. How did Jesus, the offspring of Eve, crush the head of the serpent? _____
_____
_____
_____
_____

3. What does the account teach us about God's regard for sin? _____
_____
_____
_____
_____
_____
_____

# Cain and Abel
## (Genesis 4)

### Thinking about God's Word

1. What is a way that Cain and Abel worshiped God? _____

2. How did Cain first show his anger after God did not respect his offering? _____

3. Answer this question correctly for Cain and give a reason for your answer: "Am I my brother's keeper?" _____

   _____

4. Was the mark that God set on Cain a blessing or a punishment? _____ Why?

   _____

   _____

### Working with God's Word

*Answer each question with one word or a short phrase.*

1. What name did Adam give his wife? _____

2. Who was Eve's first child? _____

3. Who was Eve's second child? _____

4. What did Cain bring as an offering to God?

   _____

5. What did Abel bring? _____

   _____

6. With whose offering was the Lord pleased?

   _____

7. Why was Cain cursed? _____

   _____

8. What would no longer yield crops for Cain?

   _____

9. How did the Lord protect Cain from being killed? _____

   _____

*Draw a line under the word that makes each sentence true.*

1. The name Eve means (evil—ever—mother—woman).

2. Killing is forbidden in the (Third—Fourth—Fifth—Sixth) Commandment.

3. Abel was a (farmer—carpenter—mason—shepherd).

4. Cain was a (farmer—carpenter—mason—shepherd).

5. God cursed Cain and made him a (foreigner—wanderer—beggar—sinner).

6. Adam was the (brother—mother—father—uncle) of Cain and Abel.

7. Cain (could—could not) have had his sin forgiven.

### Applying God's Word

1. Before Cain killed Abel, Cain received a warning from God. How does God's warning apply to all people? _____

   _____

   _____

   _____

   _____

   _____

   _____

2. How Did God show His love for Cain, even after Cain had sinned? _____

   _____

   _____

3. In what important way did God show His love for sinners such as you and me? _____

   _____

   _____

   _____

   _____

   _____

   _____

# 7  From Adam to Noah
## (Genesis 5)

### Thinking about God's Word

1. Which words tell that Adam's children did not have the image of God as Adam had it before the fall? _____
_____

2. When Adam died, which words of the Lord came true? See Lesson 5. _____
_____

3. The time of each firstborn son is called a generation. How many generations were there from Adam to Noah? _____
_____

4. What does it mean that "men began to call on the name of the LORD"? _____

5. Which words tell us that Enoch loved God?
_____

### Working with God's Word

*Answer each question with one word or number.*
1. How old was Adam when Seth was born? _____
2. How old did Adam live to be? _____
3. Who was Seth's first son? _____
4. Who was the oldest man who lived from Adam to Noah? _____
5. Whom did the Lord take to heaven without letting him die? _____
6. How long did Noah's father live? _____
7. How many sons did Noah have? _____

*Draw a line under the correct answer to each question.*
1. What was the age of the oldest man in the world? (905—969—912—996)
2. Who was Adam's son? (Enosh—Jared—Methuselah—Seth)
3. Who went to heaven alive? (Enosh—Enoch—Adam—Seth)
4. How many years did Adam live after Seth was born? (600—700—800—900)
5. Who was Noah's son? (Enosh—Enoch—Shem—Lamech)

6. Why did these early Bible people get so old? (They were healthy—They had good doctors—They never worked too hard—God wanted them to teach others)

### Applying God's Word

1. In what way do each of us still bear the image of Adam? _____
_____
_____

2. During whose lifetime did public worship begin?
_____
_____ How do you suppose people worshiped God from the time of Adam to that time? _____
_____
_____
_____
_____
_____

3. How did God show in the case of Enoch that He would give eternal life to those who believed in the promised Savior? _____
_____
_____
_____

# 8 The Flood
### (Genesis 6–9)

## Thinking about God's Word

1. What did the Lord see when men increased in number? _____

2. What did the Lord plan to do? _____
_____

3. How was Noah different from the other people?
_____
_____

4. What did God tell Noah to do? _____

5. How do the words "Noah did everything just as God commanded him" show that Noah believed God? _____
_____

6. Which people were saved by the ark? _____
_____
_____

7. Why can God not take pleasure in wickedness nor let evil dwell with Him? _____

## Working with God's Word

*Answer each question with one word, a number, or a short phrase.*

1. What happened to people as they began to increase in number? _____
_____

2. What did the Lord say He would do with people? _____
_____

3. What did the Lord tell Noah to build? _____

4. How many days and nights did it rain? _____

5. How many days did the water stay on earth?
_____

6. What did Noah do after he left the ark?
_____

7. What did the Lord place in the sky as a sign that He would not send another flood to destroy the whole earth? _____

*Answer each question.*

1. Did God send a flood to destroy the world because the people were wicked?   Yes   No

2. Did it rain for 50 days and 50 nights?   Yes   No

3. Were the mountains covered with water?
Yes   No

4. Did the water remain on the earth 150 days?
Yes   No

5. Did the ark come to rest on Ararat?   Yes   No

6. Were all people and all animals destroyed by the flood?   Yes   No

7. Does God punish wickedness today?   Yes   No

## Applying God's Word

1. Why was Noah declared righteous before God? See Hebrews 11:7. _____
_____
_____
_____

2. Which blessing that God first gave to Adam and Eve did He now give again to Noah and his family? _____
_____
_____

3. The great flood reminds us of the Sacrament of Holy Baptism. See 1 Peter 3:18–22. Explain.

_____
_____
_____
_____
_____

# 9 The Tower of Babel
## (Genesis 11)

### Thinking about God's Word

1. What did people decide to do instead of spreading out over the earth? _____ _____ _____

2. What sins did the people commit by saying the following:

   a. "Come, let us build ourselves a city"? _____ _____

   b. "Let us build ourselves a tower that reaches to the heavens"? _____ _____

   c. Let us "make a name for ourselves"? _____ _____ _____

3. How and why did God confuse the people? _____ _____ _____ _____

4. How did the changing of languages keep the people from building their city and tower? _____ _____ _____ _____

### Working with God's Word

*Fill in the blanks.*

1. The whole _____ had one language.

2. The people said to each other, "Let us build ourselves a _____ with a tower."

3. They said, "Let us make a _____ for ourselves."

4. God said, "Let Us go down and confuse their _____."

5. So the Lord _____ them.

*Fill in the blanks with words from below.*

1. These people found a _____ where they wished to stay.

2. The _____ was displeased with the people.

3. The Lord punished the people by changing their _____

4. The Lord scattered them over the face of the _____.

5. The people of Babel were _____.

   earth        language

   plain        proud        Lord

### Applying God's Word

1. Which pronoun reminds us that our God is triune—three persons in one Godhead? _____ _____ _____ _____

2. How did the people of Babel transgress God's commandments? _____ _____What was their punishment? _____ _____ _____

3. Not all pride is sinful. What is wrong with the pride of the people of Babel? See 1 Corinthians 1:30–31. _____ _____ _____ _____ _____ _____ _____

18

# 10 The Call of Abram
## (Genesis 12)

### Thinking about God's Word

1. What command came to Abram, whom God later named Abraham, from the Lord? _____
   _____

2. Where did God want Abraham to go? _____
   _____ What did
   Abraham have to leave behind? _____
   _____

3. What threefold promise did God give with His command? _____
   _____
   _____
   _____
   _____

4. Which of these promises meant the same as the promise given to Adam and Eve after the fall?
   _____
   _____

5. Which words show that Abraham believed God and did what He said? _____
   _____

6. How did Abraham worship God in public after he arrived in Canaan? _____
   _____

7. How did the Lord answer him when Abraham said that he was still childless? _____
   _____
   _____

8. Why did it take great faith on Abraham's part to believe this promise? _____
   _____

9. What does it mean to have faith in God? _____
   _____
   _____
   _____

### Working with God's Word

*Answer each question.*

1. When God called Abraham out of his homeland, which persons went with Abraham? _____
   _____

2. Near which city did Lot pitch his tent? _____

3. How old was Abraham when God came to him another time? _____

4. Who gave Abraham faith? _____

5. How did God call you and give you faith?
   _____
   _____

*Answer each question with a word from below.*

1. Who was Abraham's nephew? _____

2. Which word tells that Abraham had no children?
   _____

3. Which word means family? _____

4. Which city was filled with wicked men and sinners? _____

5. Which word tells that Abraham had faith?
   _____

| | | | |
|---|---|---|---|
| household | Shem | Sodom | believed |
| Ur | childless | Lot | Jordan |

### Applying God's Word

1. In what way have all people on earth been blessed through Abraham? _____
   _____
   _____
   _____

2. In addition to Abraham's actual descendants, who else is included among the children of Abraham? See Galatians 3:29. _____
   _____
   _____
   _____

3. Abraham believed the Lord, and He credited it to him as righteousness. How is God's righteousness credited to people today? _____
   _____
   _____
   _____

# 11 The Promise of Isaac
## (Genesis 18)

## Thinking about God's Word

1. In what form did the Lord come to Abraham at the time of this story? _____
_____
_____

2. For what special purpose had the Lord come to Abraham? _____
_____

3. How did Sarah hear the Lord's promise, even though it was not spoken directly to her? _____
_____
_____

4. How would you answer the question "Why did Sarah laugh?" _____
_____

5. Name a promise God makes to us that has not yet been fulfilled. Do you believe it will be fulfilled? Give a reason. _____
_____
_____

## Working with God's Word

*Answer each question.*

1. Who were the three men who came to Abraham's tent? _____

2. How did Abraham show kindness toward them? _____

3. Which words show that the men accepted Abraham's invitation?_____
_____
_____

4. What foods did they have for their meal? _____
_____

5. What promise did the Lord give Abraham? _____

6. How can you tell that Sarah did not believe the promise? _____

7. Why could Sarah hardly believe that she would have a son? _____
_____

8. How did the Lord know that Sarah laughed? _____

9. Why did Sarah deny that she had laughed? _____

*Fill in each blank with a word from below.*

1. Abraham _____ to meet the men.
2. Sarah used flour to make _____.
3. A servant prepared a _____.
4. The Lord said, "Sarah your wife will have a _____."
5. Sarah _____ to herself.
6. Sarah told a _____.
7. Nothing is too _____ for the Lord.

ran          son          hard

bread        laughed      lie        calf

## Applying God's Word

1. What characteristic of God is suggested by the question "Is anything too hard for God?" _____
_____
_____
_____

2. Why can we trust God to keep all of His promises? _____
_____
_____
_____

3. In this account God took on human form to visit His people. When else did God take on human form to live among His people? See Galatians 4:4. _____
_____
_____
_____

# 12 Sodom and Gomorrah
## (Genesis 19)

## Thinking about God's Word

1. Where was Lot sitting when the angels came to him? _____

2. Where did Lot take the angels ?_____
_____

3. Which words show that Lot tried to turn the men of Sodom from their evil ways? _____
_____

4. What did the angels do to the wicked men?
_____

5. Why had the angels come to visit Lot? _____
_____

6. Whom did the angels try to save besides Lot and his wife and daughters? _____
Why were they not saved? _____
_____

7. What was destroyed? _____
Who was destroyed? _____
_____

8. Whom did Lot's wife disobey when she looked back?_____ How was she punished?
_____

9. Why were the people of Sodom and Gomorrah destroyed? See Genesis 18:20–32 and 2 Peter 2:6.
_____
_____

## Working with God's Word

*Answer each question.*
1. How did Lot show kindness to the two angels?
_____

2. What did the men of Sodom want with the angels? _____
_____

3. How did the angels show their mighty power?
_____

4. At what time of the day did Lot and his family leave the city?_____

5. What warning did the angels give to Lot and his family?_____

6. Who looked behind her against the angels' command? _____
_____

7. How was she punished? _____
_____

*Circle the answer that makes each sentence true.*
1. (Two—Three—Four—Five) angels came to visit Lot.

2. The men of Sodom who came to Lot's house were (young—old—young and old).

3. Lot called the men of the city (sinners— friends—sons-in-law—heathen).

4. The two cities were burned at (morning—evening—noon).

5. (Three—Four—Five—Six) people of Sodom were saved.

## Applying God's Word

1. What does this lesson teach us about God and His regard for sin? _____
_____
_____

2. What evidence of God's love and mercy is contained in this account? _____
_____
_____

3. Explain how this account prefigures the events of the Last Day. _____
_____
_____
_____
_____
_____
_____

# 13 The Offering of Isaac
## (Genesis 22)

## Thinking about God's Word

1. What did Abraham name his son? _____

2. How did God test Abraham? _____
_____

3. Why must God's command have been a shock to Abraham? _____
_____

    What did Abraham's faith in God move him to do just the same? _____
_____

4. In which words did the angel of the Lord tell Abraham that he had passed the test? _____
_____
_____
_____

5. What did the angel of the Lord say Abraham's blessing would be? _____
_____
_____

6. Name three ways in which Abraham's son and God's Son were the same. _____
_____
_____
_____

7. God spared Abraham's son, but what did He do with His own Son? _____
_____

## Working with God's Word

*Answer each question.*

1. Why were fire, knife, and wood taken on the journey? _____

2. How did Abraham answer Isaac's question? ____
_____
_____

3. How did Abraham show that he really meant to carry out God's command? _____
_____
_____

4. What did the angel of the Lord say to Abraham when they talked the second time?_____

_____
_____
_____

5. How can you tell that Abraham had a strong faith? _____

6. How many children did God promise Abraham?
_____

7. In whom shall all the nations of the earth be blessed? _____

*Draw a circle around Yes or No.*

1. Did God tell Abraham to take his son to the land of Moriah?   Yes   No

2. Did it take four days before they saw the place in the distance?   Yes   No

3. Did Isaac carry the wood up the mountain?
Yes   No

4. Did Abraham kill his son?   Yes   No

5. Is the angel of the Lord the same as Jesus?
Yes   No

6. Is a ram a male sheep?   Yes   No

7. Did Abraham love God more than he loved Isaac?   Yes   No

## Applying God's Word

1. How did Abraham's answer to Isaac again prove his strong faith in God? _____

    How did God fulfill what Abraham said and believed a short time later? _____
_____
_____ What Lamb did God Himself provide as an offering about 2,000 years later? _____

2. What did Abraham believe God would do to restore Isaac if Abraham would have sacrificed him? See Hebrews 11:17–19. _____
_____

3. Of what great event does Abraham's belief, referred to in item 2, remind us? _____
_____
_____

# 14 Isaac and His Family

**(Genesis 27)**

## Thinking about God's Word

1. Who was Isaac's older son? _____

2. How can you tell that Isaac intended to give the blessing to Esau? _____
_____

3. How did Rebekah try to stop that? _____
_____

4. How did Jacob lie to his father? _____
_____

## Working with God's Word

*Answer each question.*

1. How old was Isaac when he got married? _____

2. Who were Isaac's two sons? _____
_____

3. To whom did Isaac wish to give the blessing?
_____

4. How did Rebekah make Jacob's skin feel like Esau's? _____

5. From which animals did Rebekah make tasty food? _____

6. Why was it easy to fool Isaac? _____
_____

7. Which blessing did Isaac give to Jacob? _____
_____

*On the blank lines write the word from below that answers the question.*

1. What did Isaac want Esau to get for him? _____

2. How many goats did Rebekah use to get meat ready for Isaac? _____

3. When Jacob came into his father's room, who did he say he was? _____

4. Whose voice did Isaac think he heard when Jacob was in the room? _____

5. Whose hands did Isaac think he felt when Jacob was in the room? _____

| Esau | food | Esau's | |
| three | two | Jacob's | Abraham |

## Applying God's Word

1. How did Jacob break each of the following commandments:

   a. Honor your father and your mother. _____

   b. You shall not steal. _____
   _____
   _____

2. Of what was Rebekah guilty? _____
_____
_____
_____
_____

3. What does Jesus' life, death, and resurrection mean for all repentant sinners? _____
_____
_____
_____
_____

# 15 Jacob's Stairway
## (Genesis 28)

## Thinking about God's Word

1. Where had Esau been while Jacob was receiving the blessing from his father? _____

2. Which words of his blessing do you think led Esau to hate his brother and want to kill him? _____

3. How did God appear to Jacob after he fled? _____

4. In which words did the Lord give Jacob a blessing? _____
_____
_____
_____

5. What three names did Jacob give to the place where he had his dream? _____
_____

6. What vow did Jacob make before he left Bethel? _____
_____

7. Have you ever been blessed by someone? When? Where? How? Why? _____
_____
_____

## Working with God's Word

*Answer each question.*

1. What did Esau intend to do to his brother? _____

2. To what place did Rebekah tell Jacob to flee? _____

3. Who stood at the top of the stairway in Jacob's dream? _____

4. What name did Jacob give to the place where he dreamed? _____

5. What were the two main parts of Jacob's vow to God for His protection? _____
_____
_____
_____
_____

*Answer these questions with names from below.*

1. Who said, "Bless me, too, my father"? _____

2. Who said, "I will give you and your descendants the land on which you are lying"? _____

3. Who said, "You will live by the sword"? _____

4. Who said, "This is none other than the house of God"? _____

5. Who said, "This is the gate of heaven"?_____

6. Who said, "I am your son, your firstborn"? _____

7. Who said, "Flee at once to my brother Laban"? _____

| God | Rebekah | Jacob |
| Esau | Isaac | Laban |

## Applying God's Word

1. Jacob received the blessing God gave to Abraham. What was the most significant part of that blessing? _____
_____

2. In what ways do God's angels serve His people? _____
_____
_____

3. How is Bethel like a Christian church? _____
_____
_____
_____
_____
_____
_____
_____
_____

# 16 Jacob's Family
## (Genesis 37)

## Thinking about God's Word

1. How many wives did Jacob have? _____

2. How many years did Jacob stay in Haran? _____ Which words show that God gave him many gifts while he was there? _____ _____

3. Which words show that God wanted Jacob to return to Canaan? _____ _____ _____

4. Why did Jacob not have to fear the long journey back to Canaan with his family? _____ _____

5. Do you think Jacob made a mistake in his love for his sons? _____ Why or why not? _____ _____ _____

6. Which words tell how Joseph's brothers felt about him? _____ _____

7. Which words show that the brothers and the father understood the meaning of Joseph's dreams? _____ _____ _____

## Working with God's Word

*Answer each question.*

1. For whom did Jacob serve Laban for 14 years? _____

2. How many years did Jacob work to earn cattle for himself ? _____

3. Why did Jacob return to Canaan with his family? _____ _____

4. How many sons did Jacob have? _____

5. How did Jacob show his great love for Joseph? _____ _____

6. What did the dreams mean? _____ _____

7. What were the names of Jacob's sons? _____ _____ _____ _____

*Draw a circle around Yes or No.*

1. Did Joseph have 12 brothers?
   Yes   No

2. Did Joseph feed the flock with his brothers?
   Yes   No

3. Did Joseph make a beautiful robe?   Yes   No

4. Did Jacob say, "You shall indeed reign over us"?
   Yes   No

5. Did Jacob scold Joseph for his dreams?   Yes   No

## Applying God's Word

1. Why do jealousy and strife exist even among the people of God? _____ _____ _____

2. How is Jacob as a father like our Father in heaven? How is he different? _____ _____ _____ _____ _____ _____ _____

3. Jacob gave Joseph a beautiful robe to wear. With what are those who have been baptized in Christ clothed (Galatians 3:27)? _____ _____ _____

# 17 Joseph and His Brothers

## (Genesis 37)

### Thinking about God's Word

1. How do the words of Jacob (Israel) to Joseph show that he wanted to be a God-pleasing father? _____ _____

2. What name did the brothers call Joseph? _____ Explain why "name-calling" is a sin against the Fifth Commandment. _____ _____ _____

3. What did the brothers do after they threw Joseph into a cistern? _____ How did this show their hard-heartedness? _____ _____ _____

4. How did the brothers deceive their father? _____ _____ _____ _____ _____

5. Show how from this lesson the brothers hurt Joseph, Jacob, and most of all themselves. Which words of Jacob tell how deeply he was hurt? _____ _____ _____ _____ _____ _____

### Working with God's Word

*Answer each question.*

1. Where did Jacob's sons go to feed the flocks? _____

2. Whom did Jacob send to see how the brothers were doing? _____

3. Who suggested that Joseph be thrown into a cistern? _____

4. Which brother suggested selling Joseph? _____

5. Who bought Joseph from the brothers? _____

6. How many shekels of silver were paid for Joseph? _____

7. How did Jacob show that he believed the brother's lie? _____ _____

*Fill in the blank spaces with words from below.*

1. The brothers said, "Let's _____ him."

2. _____ tried to rescue Joseph.

3. They _____ Joseph of his robe.

4. _____ said, "Come, let's sell him."

5. They sold him to the _____.

6. Reuben _____ his clothes when he saw the empty cistern.

7. Jacob said, "Some ferocious animal has _____ him."

| Reuben | tore | stripped |
|--------|------|----------|
| Ishmaelites | Judah | kill |
| devoured | | |

### Applying God's Word

1. Use this story to explain how sin sometimes escalates into other sins. _____ _____ _____ _____

2. Reuben pleaded with his brothers for Joseph's life. Who pleads with God on our behalf? _____ _____ _____ _____

3. How were Jesus and Joseph alike? How were they not alike? _____ _____ _____ _____ _____

# 18 Joseph Serves Pharaoh
## (Genesis 41)

## Thinking about God's Word

1. Why did Pharaoh have to find someone in place of his magicians to interpret his dreams? _____
   _____

2. How did Pharaoh know that Joseph could interpret dreams? (See Genesis 41:9–13.) _____
   _____

3. How did Joseph show his humility as he stood before Pharaoh? _____
   _____
   _____
   _____
   _____

4. In which words did Joseph give all honor and glory to God? _____
   _____

5. What advice did Joseph give Pharaoh together with the interpretation? _____
   _____
   _____
   _____
   _____
   _____
   _____

## Working with God's Word

*Answer each question with one word or a short phrase.*
1. Who had dreams in this lesson? _____
2. How many cows did Pharaoh see coming from the water? ____
3. What kind of grain grew on the stalks Pharaoh saw in his dream? _____
4. Whom did Pharaoh first ask to interpret his dreams? _____
5. According to Joseph, who alone could answer Pharaoh's dreams? _____
6. How many years of plenty and famine would there be? _____
7. Whom did Pharaoh choose as one discerning and wise? _____

8. Throughout which land did Joseph travel?
   _____
9. What did he collect?_____

*Underline the word that makes each sentence true.*
1. Pharaoh was the (king—captain—president—prince) of Egypt.
2. Pharaoh's dreams told about (14—7—10—16) years of famine.
3. Joseph said that (he—magicians—Jacob—God) would answer Pharaoh.
4. Pharaoh put Joseph in charge of (Egypt—Israel—food—people).
5. Joseph gathered (one-fifth—one-half—all—one-sixth) of the crops during the seven years of plenty.

## Applying God's Word

1. How did Joseph rise from slave and prisoner to ruler of Egypt?_____
   _____
2. What words of Joseph indicate his faith in God?
   _____
   _____
3. What did Pharaoh recognize about Joseph that made Joseph an ideal candidate for a position of authority in Egypt? _____
   _____
   _____
   _____

# 19 The Journeys of Joseph's Brothers
## (Genesis 42–43)

## Thinking about God's Word

1. How can you tell that there was a famine also in Canaan during the lean years? _____
_____

2. What news had Jacob received from Egypt? _____
_____

3. How did Joseph treat the brothers when they came to him? _____
_____

4. According to the words of Jacob, who alone could grant mercy? _____

5. Why did Joseph weep? _____
_____

6. How can you tell that Joseph still remembered all of his brothers? _____
_____

7. Why do you suppose Joseph gave Benjamin a greater portion of goods than the others? _____
_____
_____

## Working with God's Word

*Answer each question.*

1. Where was there plenty of grain? _____

2. Why did Jacob need grain from Egypt _____
_____

3. Whom did Jacob send to get the grain? _____

4. Which brother did Joseph want to see?
_____

5. Whom did Joseph order bound? _____

6. Why did the father not want Benjamin to go to Egypt? _____
_____

7. What would happen to Jacob if something happened to Benjamin? _____

*Fill in the blank spaces with words from below.*

1. Ten of Joseph's _____ went to buy grain.

2. They _____ down to Joseph.

3. Joseph turned away from them and began to
_____ .

4. Joseph gave orders to get _____ for his brothers.

5. Joseph's brothers _____ with him.

| ate | brothers | bowed |
|-----|----------|-------|
| grain | weep | true | guilty |

*Answer each question with one word or a phrase.*

1. Where did Jacob ask his sons to go again a second time? _____

2. When did Joseph want his brothers to eat with him? _____

3. How did Joseph show that he loved Benjamin?
_____
_____

4. Who got five measures of food? _____

5. What did Joseph command to be put into Benjamin's sack beside the grain? _____

*Circle Yes or No.*

1. Did Jacob say, "I have heard that there is grain in Egypt"? Yes No

2. Did Joseph's brothers recognize him? Yes No

3. Were Joseph's brothers invited for supper?
Yes No

4. Was Jacob still alive at this time? Yes No

5. Did Benjamin get four times as much as his brothers? Yes No

## Applying God's Word

1. How could Joseph easily have taken revenge on his brothers for having sold him? _____
_____
_____ Why didn't he? _____
_____

2. How does Judah's regard for his brother remind you of Jesus' love for you? _____
_____
_____
_____

3. God knows each of us even better than Joseph knew his brothers. Explain. See also Matthew 10:30. _____
_____
_____

# 20 Joseph Makes Himself Known to His Brothers

**(Genesis 44–45)**

## Thinking about God's Word

1. Of what did the steward accuse the brothers?

_____

2. How can you tell from the answer of the brothers that they were sure none of them had done the wrong? _____

_____

_____

_____

3. Why did the brothers all return to the city when the guilty one was found? _____

_____

_____

4. Whom only did Joseph say he wanted to keep as a servant? _____ Why?

_____

_____

5. How did the words of Judah show that his heart was changed? _____

_____

6. How can you tell that this is what Joseph had hoped for in testing his brothers? _____

_____

_____

7. Why were the brothers afraid at first? _____

_____

## Working with God's Word

*Answer each question.*

1. What did Joseph command his steward to do? ___

_____

2. How did the brothers show sorrow and repentance? _____

_____

3. How did Judah keep his promise to Jacob? _____

_____

_____

4. What did Joseph tell the brothers after he heard Judah? _____

5. Why were the brothers afraid of Joseph? _____

_____

6. What did Joseph say to prove that he still trusted God? _____

_____

7. How did Joseph want to take care of his father and brothers? _____

_____

*Draw a line under the correct answer to each question.*

1. Who had taken the cup from Joseph? (Benjamin—Judah—Reuben—no one)

2. Who wanted to take Benjamin's place and become a slave? (Reuben—Simeon—Judah)

3. What did Judah call Joseph? (king—brother—lord—ruler)

4. Whom did Joseph kiss? (only Benjamin—only Reuben—only Simeon—all the brothers)

5. How did Joseph show that he was a true child of God? (He wept—He nourished—He forgave—He supplied)

6. Which of the brothers was dearest to Joseph's heart? (Benjamin—Reuben—Judah—Simeon)

7. How did Joseph reward evil? (with evil—with good)

## Applying God's Word

1. What did Joseph say and do to show his brothers that he forgave them? _____

_____

_____

2. Which words show that Joseph honored God as much now as he did when he was in trouble?

_____

_____

3. Why did Joseph forgive his brothers? Read Colossians 3:13. _____

_____

# 21  Jacob and Joseph Are Reunited

## (Genesis 46–50)

### Thinking about God's Word

1. Why did Joseph send carts to Canaan? _____
_____

2. In his parting words to his brothers, how did Joseph show that he was a good brother? _____
_____

3. What did Jacob say when he was finally convinced that Joseph was alive? _____
_____
_____
_____

4. How can you tell that Jacob was happy and at peace after he saw Joseph? _____
_____

5. Why did the brothers ask Joseph to forgive their trespasses again after their father died? _____
_____
_____ What was Joseph's answer? _____
_____

### Working with God's Word

*Answer each question with one word or a phrase.*

1. How many shekels of silver did Joseph give to Benjamin? _____

2. To whom did the brothers bring the good news? _____

3. Whom did Jacob send before him to meet Joseph? _____

4. What kind of cart did Joseph use to meet his father? _____

5. Who was afraid after Jacob died? _____ _____

6. What did they ask of Joseph? _____
_____
_____

7. Who intended everything for good? _____

*Fill in the blank spaces with words from below.*

1. Joseph gave each brother new _____.

2. The silver and clothing were signs of Joseph's _____.

3. When Jacob saw Joseph again, he was ready to _____.

4. Joseph went to meet his father in a _____.

5. Joseph settled his _____ and brothers in Egypt.

6. Jacob called his sons and _____ them before he died.

7. After Jacob had died, the brothers sent word to Joseph and asked him to _____ them.

| clothes | forgive | die | |
|---|---|---|---|
| father | love | Judah | |
| hate | blessed | chariot | multiplied |

### Applying God's Word

1. Why was it better for Jacob to go to Egypt to live with Joseph than for Joseph to go to Canaan to live with Jacob? _____
_____

2. How did Joseph's answer and his action again show his faith in God and his love for the brothers? _____
_____

3. Read Romans 8:28. What things seemed evil in Joseph's life? _____
_____

How did God work for good in all things?
_____
_____
_____

# 22 The Birth of Moses

## (Exodus 1–2)

### Thinking about God's Word

1. How did the Lord bless the family of Israel in Egypt?_____
   Why didn't the new pharaoh like this?_____
   _____ How did he try to "deal shrewdly with them"?_____
   _____
   _____
   _____

2. How do you explain the fact that "the more they were oppressed, the more they multiplied"?_____
   _____
   _____ Of which blessing of God to Abraham are you reminded?_____
   _____
   _____

3. Why did Pharaoh want the baby boys drowned?
   _____
   _____

4. Think of two good reasons why the Levite woman did not drown her son. _____
   _____ Why did she not keep him at home longer?_____
   _____ Why did she place him by the river?_____
   _____
   _____
   _____
   _____

5. Was it merely by chance that the baby's sister was there when the princess came to bathe?_____
   How were the mother and daughter wise?
   _____
   _____
   _____
   _____ What did God have to do with their wisdom?_____
   _____

6. Why did the princess keep the baby she had found?_____
   _____

7. Who gave Moses his name?_____
   _____ Exodus 2:10 will tell you what it means. _____
   _____

### Working with God's Word

*Answer each question.*

1. Whom did the king not know about?_____
2. How did the king hope to crush the Israelites?
   _____
3. What very cruel law did he make?_____
   _____
4. Which mother did not obey this law?
   _____
5. What did she make in which to hide her son?
   _____
6. What did the mother do with the baby after three months?_____
   _____
7. Who came to the river to bathe?_____
   _____
8. Whom did the baby's sister call as nurse? _____
   _____
9. Why did Moses have to flee from Pharaoh?
   _____

*Fill in the blanks with the words from the following page.*

1. A _____ woman had a baby boy.
2. Pharaoh ordered, "Every _____ that is born you must throw into the Nile."
3. Moses' mother made him a basket out of _____
4. The baby's _____ stood at a distance and watched.
5. Pharaoh's daughter saw a _____ among the reeds.
6. The baby's sister asked, "Shall I go and get one of the Hebrew women to _____ the baby for you?"
7. And the _____ went and got the baby's mother.

8. Moses saw an _____ beating a Hebrew.

basket

girl

Levite

papyrus

Egyptian

sister

nurse

Moses

Hebrew boy

## Applying God's Word

1. Who became Moses' grandfather by adoption? _____ How did it benefit Moses to live in the palace of the king rather than to live at home with his family?_____

   _____

   _____ How could it have been harmful?_____

   _____

   _____

2. What evidence does this story provide to indicate that Moses identified himself with the people of God rather than with the Egyptians?_____

   _____

   _____

   _____

3. Compare Jesus' birth and the birth of Moses.

   _____

   _____

   _____

   _____

   _____

   _____

   _____

# 23 The Call of Moses
## (Exodus 3–4)

## Thinking about God's Word

1. How did the Lord appear to Moses?_____
_____
_____

2. Why did the Lord call the Hebrews "My people"?
_____
_____

 Why did the Lord want to help His people?
_____
_____

3. Which words show that Moses did not think himself great enough to lead God's people out of Egypt?_____
_____
_____

4. How did God tell Moses that He would help him?_____
_____

5. What was Moses' second excuse?_____
_____

6. What power did God give Moses to overcome that excuse?_____
_____

7. How did the Lord patiently answer the third excuse of Moses?_____
_____

## Working with God's Word

*Answer each question with one word or a short phrase.*
1. To which mountain did Moses come?_____
2. Where did the angel of the Lord appear to Moses?_____
3. Where were the Lord's people?_____
_____
4. To whom did God wish to send Moses?
_____
5. Who said He would be with Moses?_____
6. What did Moses' staff turn into?_____
7. Where did Moses put his hand?_____
_____

8. What would become of the water poured on dry ground?_____
9. Who would speak for Moses?_____

*Draw a circle around the word or phrase that answers each question.*
1. Where were the Lord's people in misery? (Egypt—Canaan—Midian—Sinai)
2. How many excuses did Moses make to God? (1—2—3—4)
3. What turned into a snake? (Moses' hand—Moses' staff—Moses' shoes—Moses' sheep)
4. Where did the Lord tell Moses to put his hand? (in his pocket—over his heart—inside his coat—on the rod)
5. What disease came over Moses' hand? (leprosy—rheumatism—measles—palsy)
6. From where should Moses take water in Egypt? (river—well—lake—fountain)
7. Who could speak well? (Aaron—Moses—a priest—Pharaoh)

## Applying God's Word

1. Why did the Lord become angry?_____
_____

2. How did living in the palace of Pharaoh prepare Moses for this work?_____
_____
_____

3. Who are the leaders of God's people today? _____
_____
_____What do we believe about their work? _____
_____
_____
_____

# 24  The Passover
## (Exodus 11–12)

## Thinking about God's Word

1. How did Moses and Aaron tell Pharaoh that they were sent by God?_____

_____

2. Whom did Pharaoh consider greater than the Lord?_____

3. Why didn't the miracles have any effect on Pharaoh's heart?_____

_____

4. List all the directions the Lord told Moses to give His people about the Passover. _____

_____

_____

_____

_____

_____

_____

_____

_____

5. What would keep death from coming over the firstborn of the children of Israel?_____

_____

## Working with God's Word

*Fill in the blanks.*

1. Moses and _____ talked to Pharaoh.

2. Pharaoh asked, "Who is the _____, that I should obey Him?"

3. The Lord had brought nine _____ upon Egypt.

4. The Lord said, "Take a lamb without _____."

5. "And slaughter it at _____."

6. "The blood will be a _____ for you on the houses."

7. "This is a day you are to _____."

8. The Israelites _____ just what the Lord commanded.

*Draw a line under the word or phrase that makes each sentence true.*

1. (Moses—Aaron—Israel—God) hardened Pharaoh's heart.

2. The children of Israel were to put blood on the (windows—doors—doorframes—steps) of their homes.

3. The children of Israel were commanded to eat (the best parts—all—as much as they cared for—most) of the Passover lamb.

4. God was going to pass through Egypt (at night—in the morning—in the afternoon—at noon).

5. The Lord was going to strike down all the (firstborn—youngest—girls—boys) in Egypt.

## Applying God's Word

1. How were the children of Israel to remember this day in future generations?_____

_____ What was the feast called?_____

2. How did the children of Israel show that they believed the Lord? _____

_____

3. Who is our Passover lamb?_____ How did He become a Passover lamb for us? See 1 Corinthians 5:7. _____

_____

# 25 The Departure from Egypt
## (Exodus 12–14)

### Thinking about God's Word

1. Why was there loud wailing in Egypt?_____
_____
_____

2. When did Pharaoh call Moses and Aaron?_____
_____ Why did the Egyptians now want the Israelites to leave quickly?
_____
_____

3. Why did Pharaoh want the Israelites back?____
_____
_____

4. What did Moses say to the people?_____
_____
_____
_____
_____
_____
_____

5. What miracle did God perform through Moses to enable the people to cross the Red Sea?_____
_____
_____

6. What do you suppose the Egyptians thought when they rushed into the Red Sea after the children of Israel?_____
_____ How did the Lord finally punish proud Pharaoh and his army in which he trusted? _____
_____

7. How did the Israelites thank God for His wonderful deliverance? See Exodus 15:1–21. _____
_____

### Working with God's Word

*Answer each question.*

1. At what time did the Lord strike down all the firstborn of Egypt?_____

2. In how many homes was at least one person dead?
_____

3. What did Pharaoh say to Moses and Aaron now?
_____
_____

4. How many men left Egypt?_____

5. How did the Lord protect His people by day and by night?_____
_____
_____

6. Where did Pharaoh's army overtake the children of Israel?_____

7. What happened to Pharaoh and his men?_____
_____

*Draw a circle around Yes or No.*

1. Did the angel of Death go through Egypt at noon?  Yes  No

2. Was Pharaoh a firstborn?  Yes  No

3. Was a person dead in every Egyptian house? Yes  No

4. Did the children of Israel travel on foot? Yes  No

5. Did the children of Israel have strong faith? Yes  No

6. Was there a wall of water on both sides of Israel? Yes  No

7. Did Pharaoh swim to shore?  Yes  No

### Applying God's Word

1. God came to His people Israel in a pillar of cloud and in a pillar of fire. How does God come to His people today?_____
_____
_____

2. God rescued His people from captivity in Egypt. From what forms of captivity has God rescued us?_____
_____

3. How and when did His rescue of us take place?
_____
_____
_____

# 26 The Giving of the Law
### (Exodus 15–16; 19–20)

## Thinking about God's Word

1. Why did the Israelites grumble? _____
_____

2. How did the Lord promise to feed them? _____
_____
_____

   How did He keep His promise? _____
_____
_____
_____

3. How did Moses tell the people to prepare themselves to meet with God? _____
_____

4. With what signs did God show the people that He had something very serious and important to tell them? _____
_____

5. Why were the people afraid? _____
_____
_____ What did they say? _____
_____
_____
_____

6. Where did God take Moses to have him receive the Law?_____

7. What are the Ten Commandments? _____
_____
_____
_____
_____
_____

## Working with God's Word

*Answer each question with a word or a short phrase.*
1. Who led Israel from the Red Sea? _____
2. Where did the children of Israel go after they left the Red Sea? _____
3. Who murmured against Moses and Aaron? ____
_____
4. What did the Lord promise Israel for twilight food? _____

5. Which bird did the Lord send for meat? _____
6. What did Israelites call the morning food?
_____
7. How long did the children of Israel eat manna?
_____
8. Where did Israel camp in the third month? ___
_____
9. What was inscribed by the finger of God? ____
_____

*Draw a line under the word that makes each sentence true.*
1. Moses led Israel from the (Dead—Red—Caspian—Black) Sea.
2. The children of Israel went into the (forest—desert—water).
3. The Israelites said they were (hungry—thirsty—tired—weak).
4. In the (first—second—third—fourth) month the Israelites came to the Desert of Sinai.
5. God wanted the people to meet Him on the (first—second—third—fourth) day.
6. Moses was on the mountain (30—40—4—50) days and nights.
7. The Ten Commandments are written in Exodus, chapter (10—20—30—40).

## Applying God's Word

1. God gave His people Israel special food. What special food has God given us? _____
_____
_____
_____

2. What does God's Law tell us? _____
_____
_____
_____

3. How did Jesus fulfill God's Law for us? _____
_____
_____

# 27 The Golden Calf
## (Exodus 32; 34)

## Thinking about God's Word

1. Why did the children of Israel become impatient with Moses? _____ _____

2. How did the people worship the idol that Aaron had made? _____ _____ _____ Why was that a sin? _____ _____

3. What did God say to Moses when He saw the people sin? _____ _____ _____ What had God always called these people before? _____ _____

4. What did Moses carry with him on the way down from the mount? _____ _____ Whose writing were they? _____

5. When did Moses get angry? _____ _____ _____ How did he show his anger? _____ _____ What did he make the people do with the idol? _____ _____ _____

6. With which words did Moses call the people to repentance? _____ _____ _____ _____

7. How did Moses again get two tablets of stone with the Ten Commandments written on them? _____ _____ _____ _____

## Working with God's Word

*Answer each question.*

1. Whom did the people ask to make gods for them? _____

2. What metal did Aaron use to make the image? _____

3. What kind of people did God say the Israelites were? _____

4. Who made the first two tablets of stone? _____

5. Who wrote the commandments on the second two tablets of stone? _____

*Fill in the blanks with words from below.*

1. _____ asked the people to bring their earrings.

2. The people made _____ offerings to the golden idol.

3. When Moses saw the dancing and the calf, he became _____.

4. The _____ wrote the Ten Commandments.

5. The people sinned against the _____ Commandment.

| Lord | burnt | Sinai | |
| Aaron | First | angry | Levi |

## Applying God's Word

1. How does this account illustrate the saying "Idle hands are the devil's workshop"? _____ _____ _____ _____ _____

2. What forms of idolatry find their way into our lives today? _____ _____ _____

3. Moses pleaded with God to forgive the people of their sins. Who pleads with God on our behalf? _____ _____

# 28 The Bronze Snake
## (Numbers 13–14; 21)

## Thinking about God's Word

1. Why did God command Moses to send men into the land before the children of Israel went in? ____
_____

2. When they returned, what did the explorers report to Moses?_____
_____ Why didn't they think the new land could be taken? _____
_____

3. What did the Israelites say? _____
_____
_____
_____ How did they again show their lack of trust in God? _____
_____

4. Who did not agree with the other explorers? _____ In whom did they trust? _____

5. How long did the Lord say the Israelites would wander? _____

6. How many Israelites did the Lord want to bring into the land of Canaan? _____ Why didn't all of them get there? _____
_____
_____
_____

7. How was the serpent a type of Christ? Think of these things: lowly, despised, set upon a pole, lifted up, looked upon, lived. _____
_____

## Working with God's Word

*Answer each question with one word.*
1. Which desert did the children of Israel leave? _____

2. Which land did the Lord want the men to search? _____

3. How did the explorers describe the people of the land? _____

4. Where did the children of Israel wish they had died? _____

5. What did the people want to use to kill the two God-fearing explorers? _____

6. What did the Lord send among the people to punish them? _____

7. Who prayed for the people? _____

*Draw a line under the word or phrase that answers the questions.*
1. After how many days did the explorers return from Canaan? (20—30—40—50)

2. Which words show that the land was a good land? (grasshoppers—milk and honey—fruit trees—grapes)

3. Who of the older Israelites would get into Canaan? (Moses—Miriam—Joshua—Aaron)

4. Who sent venomous snakes among the people? (God—Moses—Joshua—Caleb)

5. Of what was the serpent made that Moses set upon a pole? (iron—tin—clay—bronze)

6. Through what did God save the people who were dying from snakebites? (bronze snake—Moses' staff—the cross—medicine)

## Applying God's Word

1. Describe Joshua and Caleb in the face of what many would consider an overwhelming obstacle.
_____
_____
_____
_____

2. The serpent on the pole brought restored healing to all who gazed upon it. What did Jesus bring when He was lifted up on the cross? See John 3:14–15. _____
_____
_____

3. How would the 40 years in the wilderness remind the people of their sin? What knowledge of God's grace did the people possess during their 40 years of wandering? _____
_____
_____
_____
_____
_____
_____

## 29 Israel Enters Canaan
### (Deuteronomy 34; Joshua 1–5)

### Thinking about God's Word

1. Just as Israel was about to enter Canaan, what did the Lord show Moses from Mount Nebo? _____ _____ What happened to Moses then? _____ Why does no one know where the grave of Moses is? _____ _____

2. Why did the Lord not permit His servant Moses to go into the Promised Land? See Numbers 20:7–12. _____ _____

3. List the directions God gave the new leader. _____ _____ _____ _____ _____ _____ How would he be successful? _____ _____

4. When the people were ready to enter the land, who went first? _____ Why was this proper? _____ _____

5. How was it possible for the Israelites to pass over the Jordan on dry ground? _____ _____

6. When did the waters of the Jordan flow as before? _____

7. Why did the manna now stop falling from heaven? _____ _____

### Working with God's Word

*Fill in the blanks.*

1. The Israelites grieved for Moses _____ days.

2. God told Joshua, "Do not let this Book of the _____ depart from your mouth."

3. The priests carried the _____ _____

4. The water flowing down to the _____ Sea was cut off.

5. Upon entering the Promised Land the people ate some unleavened bread and _____.

*Draw a line under the word or phrase that makes each sentence true.*

1. (Joshua—The children of Israel—The Lord—Aaron) buried Moses.

2. (Caleb—Aaron—Joshua—Moses) was chosen by God to lead the children of Israel into Canaan.

3. Joshua said, "(Three—Four—Five—Six) days from now you will cross the Jordan."

4. The Israelites had to cross the (Salt Sea—Jordan—Red Sea—Nile) to get into the Promised Land.

### Applying God's Word

1. Through what means did God promise to make Joshua prosperous and successful? _____ _____ _____

2. God told Joshua that He would remain with him wherever he would go. How did God dramatically show His presence? _____ _____ _____ _____

3. What are some promises God has made to you? How can you be sure that God will keep them? _____ _____ _____ _____

# 30 The Conquest of Canaan

## (Joshua 6–10)

## Thinking about God's Word

1. How did the children of Israel show their faith in God's plan to take Jericho? _____

_____

_____

2. What happened to Jericho? _____

_____

3. By what miracle did the Lord make a complete victory possible? _____

_____

## Working with God's Word

*Answer the questions.*

1. How many days were the armed men to go around the city one time? _____

2. When were the armed men of war to circle the city seven times? _____

3. What noise did the people make on the seventh day? _____

4. Why was it easy for the Israelites to go into the city? _____

5. Why did Joshua not have to fear the five kings of the Amorites? _____

_____

_____

*Answer each question with Yes or No.*

1. Did the Israelites walk around Jericho 13 times?
   Yes   No

2. Did the armed men blow their trumpets?
   Yes   No

3. Did it take two weeks to capture Jericho?
   Yes   No

4. Did five kings of the Amorites join forces against Israel?   Yes   No

5. Did Joshua say, "O sun, stand still"?   Yes   No

6. Did the Lord give Israel the land of their forefathers?   Yes   No

7. Was Joshua the leader of Israel?   Yes   No

## Applying God's Word

1. In what three ways did God act to give His people victory? _____

_____

_____

_____

2. What "walls" has God broken down for you? _____

_____

_____

_____

_____

_____

_____

3. How can you tell that the Lord provided Israel with everything they needed in the Promised Land? _____

_____

_____ Which promise of God to Abraham was now completely fulfilled? _____

_____ Which greater promise was not yet fulfilled? _____

_____

# 31 Gideon

## (Judges 6)

### Thinking about God's Word

1. After the Lord had mercifully brought the children of Israel back to Canaan, what did they do?
_____
_____

2. How did the Lord punish them? _____
_____
_____

3. How did the Midianites hurt Israel? _____
_____
_____

4. How did Israel show that they were sorry for what they had done? _____
_____

5. What did the Lord want Gideon to do? _____
_____

6. Why did the Lord want the army of Israel reduced to 300? _____
_____
_____
_____

7. In the words of their battle cry, how did Gideon's men show that they believed God would help them? _____
_____

### Working with God's Word

*Answer each question with one word or a short phrase.*

1. What did the children of Israel do in the eyes of the Lord? _____

2. Into whose hands did the Lord deliver Israel?
_____

3. Where was Gideon threshing wheat? _____
_____

4. Who appeared to Gideon? _____
_____

5. Whom did Gideon send to gather the people?
_____

6. How many were afraid to fight? _____

7. How many men did the Lord use to save Israel?
_____

8. How many men were in each company? _____

9. Who won the battle? _____
_____

*Draw a line under the word or phrase that answers each question.*

1. Into whose hands did the Lord give Israel? (Philistines—Amorites—Ammonites—Midianites)

2. What was Gideon doing at the winepress? (making wine—pressing grapes —herding sheep—threshing wheat)

3. How many Israelites were afraid to fight? (22,000—300—32,000—10,000)

4. How many were used by God to defeat the Midianites? (22,000—300—32,000—10,000)

5. Into how many companies did Gideon divide his army? (1—2—3—300—4)

6. What picture does Scripture use to describe the number of Midianites in the valley? (like dogs—like locusts—like flies—like giants)

7. In which hand did the Israelites hold their torches? (left—right—both)

8. Who caused the men to turn their swords on each other? (Gideon—Midianites—Israel—God)

### Applying God's Word

1. How did God show Gideon and the soldiers that their faith was not in vain? _____
_____

2. What did Israel do when they were in trouble?
_____

3. 1 Corinthians 1:25 records, "For the foolishness of God is wiser than man's wisdom, and the weakness of God is stronger than man's strength." How does this account exemplify the truth of these New Testament words? _____
_____
_____
_____

# 32 Samson (Part 1)
### (Judges 13–14)

## Thinking about God's Word

1. Why did the Lord give Israel over to the Philistines? Read the answer in Judges 13:1.
_____
_____

2. What message did the angel of the Lord bring to Manoah's wife? _____
_____
_____

What was Manoah's son to do? _____
_____

3. Whom did Samson want permission to marry? ___
_____

Why didn't Samson's father and mother like his marriage to a Philistine girl? _____
_____ Why did the Lord permit the marriage? _____
_____
_____

4. How did Samson show his strength when a young lion came toward him? _____
_____ How can you tell that it really was not Samson who killed the lion? _____
_____
_____

5. What riddle did Samson give his companions?
_____
_____
_____ What should Samson's wife have done when the 30 men threatened to burn her and her father's household? _____
_____ What would you have done? _____
_____
_____

## Working with God's Word

_Answer each question on the blank lines._

1. What did Manoah's wife name her child?
_____

2. Where did Samson find a wife? _____
_____

3. To how many companions did Samson tell a riddle? _____

4. How did Samson's wife get the answer to the riddle? _____
_____

5. Where did Samson get the clothes to give to the men? _____

_Fill in the blanks with words from below._

1. Samson's father's name was _____

2. Samson was a _____ to the Lord.

3. The _____ of the Lord moved in Samson.

4. Samson went down to _____.

5. Samson tore apart the lion as he might have torn apart a _____.

6. Samson's riddle was answered in _____ days.

7. Samson struck down _____ men and took their clothes.

| 30 | seven | goat |
|------|--------|--------|
| Nazirite | Manoah | Timnah | Spirit |

## Applying God's Word

1. How did Samson's wife break the Sixth Commandment? _____
_____

2. What was the true source of Samson's strength?
_____

3. Compare Samson with Jesus, the ultimate Deliverer. _____
_____
_____
_____
_____
_____
_____

## 33 Samson (Part 2)
### (Judges 15–16)

### Thinking about God's Word

1. What did the Philistines do to take Samson captive? _____ _____

2. When the Philistines shouted against Samson, what do you suppose they said? _____ _____

3. What did the Philistines want Samson's wife to find out for them? _____ _____ How did they get her to find out? _____ _____

4. What did the Philistines do to Samson? _____ _____ _____

5. Why was it easy for the Philistines to bind Samson now? _____ _____

6. Read the words that show that the Philistines worshiped an idol. _____ _____ _____

7. Who gave Samson the strength to destroy the building? _____ How many people in the building were killed? _____ Which words show that Samson was killed too? _____

### Working with God's Word

*Fill in the blanks.*

1. The Philistines went up and _____ in Judah.

2. The people of Judah bound Samson with two new _____.

3. Samson struck down _____ men with the jawbone of a donkey.

4. Samson loved _____, a Philistine woman.

5. Samson said, "No _____ has ever been used on my head."

6. Delilah called a man to shave off the _____ braids of his hair.

7. The Philistines gouged out Samson's _____ and took him to Gaza.

8. On the roof of the temple there were about _____ men and women.

9. Samson took hold of the two central _____.

*Draw a line under the correct answer to each question.*

1. Why had the Philistines come to the Israelites? (to fight—to steal—to find Samson—to inspect)

2. How many shekels of silver did each of the Philistine rulers promise Delilah? (1,100—1,200—1,300—1,400)

3. Where did the Philistines put Samson when they got to Gaza? (dungeon—grave—prison—house—ward)

4. Who was the god of the Philistines? (the Lord—Baal—Dagon—Ashtoreth)

5. How many people were on the roof of the house? (30,000—3,000—300—400)

### Applying God's Word

1. What words indicate how Samson, like all people of God, received his strength? _____ _____

2. How did the Philistines break the First Commandment? How did Samson break the First Commandment? _____ _____ _____ _____

3. In his death Samson destroyed much evil. How does Samson's death remind us of the death of Jesus? _____ _____ _____ _____ _____

## 34 Ruth

### (The Book of Ruth)

### Thinking about God's Word

1. When did the famine mentioned in our lesson come over Canaan? See Ruth 1:1. _____
   _____

2. How many persons belonged to the family of Elimelech? _____

3. Whom did Elimelech's sons marry? ( _____
   _____

4. After 10 years in the land of Moab, who of Elimelech's family were still living? _____
   _____

5. To which land did Naomi now want to return? _____ What did Ruth answer when Naomi told her daughters-in-law to return to their own homes? _____
   _____
   _____
   _____

6. After the two women settled in Bethlehem, where did Ruth work to provide food for Naomi and herself? _____

7. Who was Boaz? _____
   _____ How did he show favor to Ruth?
   _____
   _____Why did he favor her?_____
   _____
   _____ Whose property did Boaz buy?
   _____

8. Who was Ruth's grandson? _____ Who was her great-grandson? _____

### Working with God's Word

*Answer each question with one word.*

1. Who took his wife and two sons to Moab?
   _____

2. Where did the wives of Mahlon and Kilion come from? _____

3. To which town did Ruth and Naomi go?
   _____

4. Who owned fields in Bethlehem? _____

5. Who became the wife of Boaz? _____

6. Who was Jesse's son?_____

7. What was the relationship of Ruth to David?
   _____

*Draw a line under the word that makes each sentence true.*

1. Naomi was the wife of (Elimelech—Mahlon—Kilion—Boaz).

2. Elimelech had (2—3—4—5) sons.

3. Naomi was Ruth's (sister-in-law—daughter-in-law—mother-in-law).

4. Naomi lived in Moab about (5—10—15—20) years.

5. (Ruth—Orpah—Delilah—Miriam) left Naomi to return to her mother's house.

6. Boaz lived in (Bethlehem—Moab—Jerusalem—Jericho).

7. (Ruth—Orpah—Naomi—Boaz) was Ruth's second husband.

### Applying God's Word

1. Ruth's words to Naomi include a beautiful confession of faith. Explain. _____
   _____

2. How does the story of Ruth show us that God's love and grace extend to all people? _____
   _____
   _____
   _____
   _____

3. Ruth became the ancestor of many kings, including King David. Who is Ruth's greatest descendant? See Matthew 1:1–5. _____
   _____

44

# 35 The Boy Samuel
## (1 Samuel 1–4)

## Thinking about God's Word

1. Read 1 Samuel 1:10–11. Why was Hannah, the wife of Elkanah, "in bitterness of soul"? _____ _____

2. To whom did she pray? _____

3. What promise did Hannah make to the Lord? _____

4. How did the Lord remember Hannah? _____ _____

5. What did Hannah name her child? _____ How did she keep her promise? _____ _____ _____

## Working with God's Word

*Answer each question.*

1. Who were Elkanah's two wives? _____ _____

2. Why did Hannah pray to the Lord? _____ _____

3. Why did Hannah bring Samuel to the house of the Lord? _____ _____

4. How was the Lord going to punish Eli and his sons? _____ _____

5. What did the Lord tell Samuel while he slept? _____ _____

6. Against whom did Israel go to battle? ____ _____

7. What happened to the Israelites? _____ _____ _____

8. What happened to Eli and his two sons? ____ _____ _____ _____

*Draw a line through the sentences that are not true.*

1. Elkanah had a wife by the name of Hannah.
2. Peninnah was the wife of Elkanah.
3. Hannah called her son Eli.
4. Eli was a good father.
5. Eli was Samuel's teacher.
6. God said to Eli, "Your two sons will both die on the same day."
7. The Philistines took the ark of God.

## Applying God's Word

1. How does this account show that children are a gift of God? _____ _____ _____ _____

2. According to the man of God, what sin did Eli commit? _____ _____

3. How did Hannah show that she loved God even more than she loved her son? _____ _____ _____ _____ _____

# 36 King Saul
## (1 Samuel 8–15)

### Thinking about God's Word

1. Who was the last judge of Israel? See 1 Samuel 7:15. _____

2. Why did the elders tell Samuel they wanted a king? _____
Why was that a sin? _____
_____

3. Why did Samuel call the tribes of Israel together? _____ Note: There were 13 tribes in Israel, one for each son of Jacob except Joseph. He was honored with two tribes named after his two sons, Ephraim and Manasseh. We usually speak of 12 tribes because the sons of Levi did not inherit a province of their own. They were the priests and as such received offerings from the other tribes.

4. How did Saul, the new king, show his humility? _____

5. Why did Saul immediately have to go to war? _____
_____ What two things made it possible for Saul to win? _____
_____
_____
_____ Why?
_____

### Working with God's Word

*Answer each question with one word or a short phrase.*

1. Who came to Samuel and asked for a king? _____
_____

2. Whom had Israel rejected? _____

3. Who was chosen as Israel's first king? _____

4. Who came upon Saul? _____
_____

5. Who won the battle against Ammon? _____
_____

6. What instructions regarding the Amalekites did God give Saul? _____
_____

7. Whose instructions did Saul say he performed?
_____

8. What had Saul spared besides the sheep? _____
_____

9. What is not as important as obedience? _____

*Of whom do you think when you read each of the following sentences?*

1. All the elders of Israel came to him. _____

2. He was displeased that Israel wanted a king.
_____

3. The first king was the son of Kish. _____

4. They shouted, "Long live the king."
_____

5. He said, "I did what the LORD wanted." _____

6. He said, "To obey is better than sacrifice."
_____

7. He rejected Saul as king. _____

### Applying God's Word

1. What does this account teach us about the relationship between God and our governing authorities?_____
_____

2. Evaluate Saul's words "I have carried out the LORD'S instructions." _____
_____
_____
_____
_____
_____
_____

3. How do God's people rightly honor Him as Lord of their lives? See Acts 5:29. _____
_____
_____
_____

## 37 David Is Chosen
### (1 Samuel 16–17)

## Thinking about God's Word

1. Why did the Lord send Samuel to Jesse?_____
   _____
   _____

2. Read the words that tell that David was blessed and Saul was plagued. _____
   _____
   _____
   _____
   _____

3. Against whom did Saul and his army have to go to battle again?_____

4. Why, do you suppose, was Goliath so eager to fight this battle alone with an Israelite?_____
   _____
   _____
   _____ In whom did the
   giant put his trust? _____
   In whom should Israel have trusted?_____
   _____

5. How did David show that he was not frightened by the giant?_____
   _____
   _____
   _____

## Working with God's Word

*Write the answers to the following questions.*
1. Who was chosen to be the next king?_____
2. How can you tell that God was with David?
   _____
3. Who gathered their armies against Israel?
   _____
4. Who was the champion of the Philistines?
   _____
5. Who was afraid of him?_____
   _____
6. How did David help his father? _____
   _____
7. What did David call the Philistine giant? _____
   _____

8. To whom were the words of David reported?
   _____

*Answer Yes or No.*
1. Did David play a violin for Saul?   Yes   No
2. Did David serve the king?   Yes   No
3. Was Goliath more than 10 feet tall?   Yes   No
4. Were Saul and his army afraid of Goliath?
   Yes   No
5. Did Goliath come forward every day for 40 days?
   Yes   No
6. Was David afraid of Goliath?   Yes   No
7. Did David trust in himself?   Yes   No

## Applying God's Word

1. How did God give David opportunity to learn the work of a king? _____
   _____
   _____

2. What evidence shows that God's Spirit was upon David? _____
   _____
   _____

3. How do the words of David's most famous psalm, Psalm 23, reflect his background as a musician, shepherd, and soldier?_____
   _____
   _____
   _____
   _____
   _____
   _____
   _____
   _____

## 38 David and Goliath
### (1 Samuel 17)

## Thinking about God's Word

1. How did David prove to Saul that he was not afraid of the giant? _____

2. Why didn't David take the armor of Saul? _____ _____

   Describe the weapons he did take. _____ _____ _____

3. Which words of Goliath show that he despised David? _____ _____

4. With what did Goliath come to David? _____ _____ In whose name did David come to Goliath? _____ _____ _____ Who was better prepared? _____ Why? _____ _____

5. How did David boldly foretell who would win? _____ _____ _____ _____ Why would God hand Goliath over to David? _____ _____

6. How did David drop the giant to the ground? _____ _____ How did David kill him? _____

7. Why did the Philistines flee? _____ _____ Why was it easy for Israel to win now? _____ _____ _____

## Working with God's Word

*Answer each question.*

1. When Goliath appeared, what did David say to Saul? _____

2. Why didn't Saul think David could win?_____ _____ _____

3. Why did David know he could win? _____ _____

4. How did Saul wish to protect David? _____ _____

5. What things did David use for weapons? _____ _____

6. What attitude did David show in his words to Goliath? _____ _____

7. Where did the stone strike the giant? _____ _____

8. How did David make sure that Goliath would die? _____

9. Who won the battle? _____

*Are the following sentences true or false?*

1. Saul commanded David to fight Goliath. T  F

2. David belonged to the army of Israel. T  F

3. With the Lord, David could not be beaten. T  F

4. David was a soldier of the Lord. T  F

5. David chose five smooth stones. T  F

6. David carried no real weapon of war. T  F

7. Goliath trusted in himself. T  F

8. Goliath trusted in his sword, shield, and spear. T  F

9. The Lord won the war for Israel. T  F

10. The First Commandment tells us to trust in God above all things. T  F

## Applying God's Word

1. What was David's answer to Saul's words? _____ _____ _____ How did David know that the Lord would deliver him? Think of what he had received from Samuel. _____ _____

2. What important lesson did David teach the army of Israel? _____

3. David faced and defeated Israel's great enemy. Some thousand years later, David's descendant defeated the greatest enemy of all people. Explain. _____ _____

48

# 39 David's Fall and Repentance

(2 Samuel 11–12)

## Thinking about God's Word

1. Who really killed Uriah? _____ Why?
_____

2. Why did the Lord send Nathan to David? ____
_____ Read what
Nathan said to him.

3. If David meant what he said about punishing the
rich man, whom would he have had to punish?
_____ How was David punished? _____
_____
_____

4. Which were David's words of repentance? _____
_____

5. In which words did Nathan announce God's forgiveness to David? _____
_____
_____

## Working with God's Word

*Answer each question with one word.*

1. Whom did Joab and his servants destroy?
_____

2. At what time of day did David walk upon the
roof of his palace? _____

3. Whose wife was Bathsheba? _____

4. Whom did David take to be his wife?
_____

5. Who was the man who took the poor man's
lamb? _____

6. What had David done against God? _____

7. Was David's sin forgiven? _____

*Fill in the blanks with words from below.*

David sent _____ to fight against Ammon and
Rabbah, while he stayed in _____. David
wanted Bathsheba's husband to _____. After Uriah
was dead, David took Bathsheba to be his _____.
David said, "I have _____ against the LORD."
David's sin was _____ but his child _____.

| Nathan | sinned | died |
|--------|--------|------|
| wife | sin | Joab |
| Jerusalem | die | forgiven |

## Applying God's Word

1. Where should David have been instead of at
home in Jerusalem ?_____ How
did Satan use David's idleness to lead him into
sin? _____
_____

2. Explain the truth about David's words after hear-
ing Nathan's story of the rich man's theft.
_____
_____
_____

3. What words reveal God's grace to David?
_____
_____
_____ Who took away David's sin and
ours? _____
_____

# 40 Absalom's Rebellion
## (2 Samuel 14–18)

## Thinking about God's Word

1. Who was Absalom? _____ For what was he praised? _____
   _____

2. What did Absalom want?_____
   _____ Why was this a sin? See Romans 13:9. _____
   _____
   _____

3. How did Absalom steal the hearts of the Israelites? _____
   _____
   _____

4. What did Absalom tell his father he wanted in Hebron? _____
   Which words showed that he wanted to start a rebellion? _____
   _____
   _____ Find the meaning of the word *rebellion* in your dictionary. _____
   _____

5. Who fled from his son? _____ Who chased after his father? _____

## Working with God's Word

*Fill in the blanks with the correct word.*
1. Absalom said, "If only I were appointed _____ in the land."
2. Absalom said that he wanted to go to Hebron to fulfill a _____.
3. David had to _____ from Absalom, his son.
4. Joab killed Absalom with three _____.
5. Absalom was buried in a _____.

*Draw a line under the word or phrase that makes each sentence true.*
1. David was Absalom's (brother—father—servant—general).
2. Absalom said he wanted to go to (Jerusalem—Jordan—Bethlehem—Hebron) to fulfill a vow.
3. Despising the government is sinning against the (Third—Fourth—Ninth—Tenth) Commandment.
4. David and his people fled across the (Nile—Kishon—Jordan—Tigris).
5. Absalom fled (on a mule—on a horse—in a chariot—in a wagon).
6. Absalom's head caught in the boughs of (a maple—a pine—an oak—a sycamore).
7. Absalom's body was covered with (earth—stones—water—grass).

## Applying God's Word

1. How did the father show his love for his son in spite of his son's unfaithfulness? _____
   _____
   _____

2. Absalom not only rebelled against his father, but he also rebelled against God. Explain. _____
   _____
   _____
   _____

3. Which commandment did Absalom clearly break? Who kept this and all other commandments for us? _____
   _____
   _____
   _____
   _____

# 41 Solomon and the Temple

## (1 Kings 3–8)

## Thinking about God's Word

1. Who was Solomon's father? _____

2. What special favor did Solomon ask for? _____
_____

3. What did the Lord give Solomon that was more than he asked for? _____
_____

4. What should Solomon do to have a long life?
_____

5. What did Solomon build? _____

6. How long did it take to build? _____

7. What did Solomon ask the Lord to do for the people of Israel? _____

## Working with God's Word

*Answer each question correctly.*

1. Who sat upon the throne of David, his father?
_____

2. How did the Lord appear to Solomon? _____
_____

3. What did the Lord give Solomon? _____
_____

4. Who said the prayer before the altar of the Lord? _____

5. What did Solomon ask the Lord to do for those who sinned against Him? _____

*Draw a line under the word or phrase that answers the question correctly.*

1. What did Solomon call himself before the Lord? (king—priest—servant—man)

2. What did Solomon pray for? (honor—riches—wisdom—a great kingdom)

3. Where was the ark of the covenant placed? (in the palace—in the Most Holy Place—in the court)

4. What name did Solomon call God in his prayer? (Jehovah—God—Almighty—Lord, God of Israel)

## Applying God's Word

1. What portion of Solomon's answer to God indicates his humility and faith? _____
_____
_____
_____
_____

2. With what action did Solomon demonstrate his love for God? _____
_____

3. How did Solomon show his concern for the sins of his people? _____
_____

Who ultimately paid for the sins of all people? How much did it cost? _____
_____
_____

# 42 The Prophet Elijah

## (1 Kings 16–17)

## Thinking about God's Word

1. Ahab was the seventh king of Israel. Which words tell that he was very wicked? _____ _____ _____

2. How did the Lord try to bring Ahab to repentance? _____

3. Why was "neither dew nor rain" a terrible punishment? _____ _____ How long would the curse last? _____ _____ Which words tell that rain would fall again only at God's command? _____ _____

4. How did the Lord take care of His servant Elijah? _____ _____ _____ Why? _____ _____

5. Why was it not only a miracle that food was brought to Elijah, but also that _____ brought the food? _____ _____

6. Why did Elijah leave the brook in the Kerith Ravine? _____

7. Why was it strange that the Lord should command a widow to feed His prophet? _____ _____ _____

8. Why was Elijah's request for water hard to grant? _____

9. Why would this widow not have to fear? _____ _____ How can you tell that she believed? _____ _____

10. How was Elijah able to bring the widow's son back from death? _____ _____

## Working with God's Word

*Fill in the blanks.*

1. Ahab sinned against God by worshiping _____.

2. _____ the prophet talked to Ahab.

3. God held back _____ from Ahab's land.

4. Ravens brought Elijah _____ and meat.

5. The Lord told Elijah to go to the city of _____.

6. A _____ took care of Elijah in this city.

7. _____ gives us all our food.

*Draw a line through the sentences that are not true.*

1. God sent rain to the earth when Ahab asked for it.

2. The Lord commanded Elijah to hide at the Kerith Ravine.

3. Ravens brought food in the morning and evening to Elijah.

4. Elijah went to the home of a widow in Zebulon.

5. Elijah gathered sticks near the village of Zarephath.

6. The Lord gave the widow money to buy food.

7. Elijah brought the widow's husband back from the dead.

## Applying God's Word

1. Of which Sacrament do the miracles of God's care for Elijah remind us? _____ _____ _____

2. How does God's care for Elijah compare with God's care for us? _____ _____

3. What other Bible accounts show God's power over death? _____ _____ _____ _____

# 43 Elijah and the Prophets of Baal
## (1 Kings 18)

## Thinking about God's Word

1. Whom were the people worshiping besides God? _____

2. How did Elijah put the idol Baal to a test? _____
   _____
   _____
   _____
   _____

3. What showed that the idol Baal had no power?
   _____

4. How did Elijah make it harder for fire to burn his altar? _____
   _____ On whom did he call? _____

5. How can you tell that the fire that fell from heaven was truly a fire sent by God? _____
   _____
   _____

6. How did the people confess that Elijah had won the test? _____
   _____
   _____

7. What did the people now do at Elijah's command? _____
   _____

## Working with God's Word

*Draw a line through the following sentences that are not taken from the story.*

1. Elijah said, "Get two bulls for us."

2. They called on Dagon all day long.

3. He repaired the altar of the Lord that was broken down.

4. Elijah took 12 stones and built an altar.

5. He dug a trench around the altar.

6. The water ran down around the altar and even filled the trench.

7. "Answer me, O LORD; answer me!"

8. Then the fire of the Lord fell and burned up the sacrifice.

*Fill in the blanks with words from below.*

_____ preached to the people. He said, "If the _____ is God, follow Him; but if _____ is God, follow him." The prophets of Baal prepared a _____. Elijah did likewise. Then the prophets of Baal called to Baal from _____ till noon. But Baal did not answer. When Elijah prayed to the Lord, fire fell from _____. It burned the bull, the wood, the stones, and the soil and licked up the _____. The people then fell down and _____ God. But Elijah took the prophets of Baal to the _____ Valley and slaughtered them.

| | | |
|---|---|---|
| heaven | Baal | LORD |
| morning | water | bull |
| praised | Kishon | fire |
| Elijah | | |

## Applying God's Word

1. Elijah exemplifies the courage God gives His people. Explain. _____
   _____
   _____
   _____

2. Why can it always be said that the power to believe comes down from heaven? _____
   _____
   _____
   _____

3. Elijah prayed to the God of Abraham, Isaac, and Israel. Is Elijah's God the same as ours? Explain.
   _____
   _____
   _____
   _____

# 44 Naboth's Vineyard

## (1 Kings 21)

### Thinking about God's Word

1. For what purpose did Ahab say he wanted Naboth's vineyard? _____ _____ How did he intend to get it? _____

2. Why would it have been a sin for Naboth to trade or sell his land? See Numbers 36:7. _____ _____ _____ _____ _____

3. How did the king act like a small child? _____ _____ _____

4. Who was Jezebel? _____ _____ What promise did she make to the king? _____ _____

5. What was her scheme for getting the vineyard? _____ _____ _____ _____

6. Why was Ahab able to take possession of the vineyard? _____

7. What was Elijah to say to Ahab? _____ _____ _____ _____ _____ _____ _____ _____

### Working with God's Word

*Answer each question.*

1. Where was Naboth's vineyard? _____ _____

2. Why couldn't Naboth sell his vineyard? _____ _____

3. Who said she would get the vineyard? _____

4. What were the false witnesses to say against Naboth? _____ _____

5. How was Naboth put to death? _____.

6. Whom did the Lord send to Ahab? _____ _____

7. Where would Ahab die? _____

8. Where and how would Jezebel die? _____ _____ _____

9. Which words say that Elijah's words came true? _____ _____

*Draw a line under the correct answer to each question.*

1. Coveting is a sin against which commandment? (Seventh—Fifth—Ninth—Eighth)

2. How had Naboth gotten his property? (bought it—earned it—inherited it—stole it)

3. To whom were the letters sent? (priests— elders—princes—soldiers)

4. False witnesses sin against which commandment? (Seventh—Fifth—Ninth— Eighth)

5. Whom did dogs eat? (Jezebel—Naboth— Elijah—Ahab)

### Applying God's Word

1. To what other sins may coveting lead, as illustrated by this Bible story? _____ _____ _____

2. What does this account show about God's attitude toward sin? _____ _____ _____

3. How did God solve the problem of human sinfulness? _____ _____

# 45 Elisha Sees Elijah Ascend
## (2 Kings 2)

## Thinking about God's Word

1. How was the Lord going to take Elijah into heaven? _____

2. Who went with Elijah to cross the River Jordan? _____ How did they get across? _____
_____
_____
_____

3. Elijah was Elisha's teacher. After Elijah ascended into heaven, Elisha was to be prophet in his place. How did Elisha's answer to his teacher show that he knew what gift he needed to serve in Elijah's place? _____
_____

4. What form of transportation did the angels of heaven use to get Elijah? _____
_____

5. Who saw this miracle? _____ What did he call after Elijah? _____
_____
_____

6. By what miracle did the Lord show Elisha that He was with him? _____
_____
_____

7. What did the prophets of Jericho now say of Elisha? _____
_____ What did they mean?
_____
How did they know? See 2 Kings 2:14–15._____
_____
_____

## Working with God's Word

*Answer each question with one word or a short phrase.*

1. Where did the Lord want to take Elijah?
_____

2. Who walked with Elijah? _____

3. With what did Elijah hit the water? _____

4. For how big a portion of Elijah's spirit did Elisha ask? _____

5. In what did Elijah ride to heaven? _____
_____
_____

*Answer each question with Yes or No.*

1. Was Elijah a true servant of God?   Yes   No

2. Did the waters part for Elijah?   Yes   No

3. Did Elijah ask for a double portion of Elisha's spirit?   Yes   No

4. Did Elijah go up by a whirlwind to heaven? Yes   No

5. Did Elisha cry, "My father! My father! The chariots and horsemen of Israel!"?   Yes   No

6. Did Elisha strike the waters with his cloak? Yes   No

7. Did the prophets live in Bethel?   Yes   No

## Applying God's Word

1. Why did Elisha refer to Elijah as his father?
_____
Who has taught you about God? _____
_____

2. How do you know that you have received the Holy Spirit (1 Corinthians 12:3)? _____
_____
_____
_____

3. Elijah preceded Elisha. Who similarly preceded Jesus to prepare the way for Him and His atoning ministry (see Luke 1:17 and John 1:29–34)?
_____
_____
_____
_____

# 46 Naaman and Elisha

## (2 Kings 5)

### Thinking about God's Word

1. Who was Naaman? _____
_____

2. What was wrong with him? _____

3. What did the servant girl say?_____
_____
_____

4. Why did Naaman take money and clothing to Samaria? _____ How did he travel? _____
_____

5. How did Elisha humble Naaman? _____
_____
_____

6. How did the servants persuade their master to try Elisha's cure? _____
_____
_____
_____ What happened? _____

7. In which words did Naaman admit that God of Israel had cured him? _____
_____
_____ How did he want to reward Elisha? _____ Why do you suppose Elisha refused the reward? _____
_____
_____

### Working with God's Word

*Fill in the blanks.*

1. _____ was commander of the army of the king of Aram.

2. _____ had leprosy.

3. A _____
served Naaman's wife.

4. Naaman was told to wash in the _____ River seven times.

5. Naaman thought the rivers of _____ were better than the rivers of Israel.

6. _____ was a servant of Elisha.

7. Naaman gave Gehazi _____ talents of silver.

8. Gehazi said to Elisha, "Your servant _____ go anywhere."

9. Gehazi became a _____.

*Draw a line through the sentences that are not true.*

1. Naaman was king of Syria.

2. A servant girl told Naaman to go to Samaria.

3. Naaman took much gold, silver, and clothing on his trip to Samaria.

4. Elisha did not go out to see Naaman when he came to Samaria to be healed.

5. Naaman dipped himself into the Jordan River six times.

6. Naaman became a believer in the true God.

7. Gehazi was Naaman's servant.

8. Gehazi was punished for coveting, lying, and deceiving.

### Applying God's Word

1. What evidence does this account provide of God's love and grace for all people? _____
_____
_____

2. What does this account teach us about God's attitude toward sin? _____
_____
_____
_____

3. Naaman's washing in the Jordan reminds us of the Baptism God offers us in Christ Jesus. Explain.
_____
_____
_____

## 47 God Sends Jonah
### (Jonah 1–3)

### Thinking about God's Word

1. Who was Jonah? _____

2. Where did the Lord tell Jonah to go? _____
_____ Why? _____
_____
_____

3. Why did Jonah get on a ship? _____
_____
_____

4. Whom was Jonah trying to get away from? _____
_____

5. What did Jonah tell the sailors to do? _____
_____

6. Where was Jonah for three days and three nights?
_____

7. How did Jonah survive? _____
_____

### Working with God's Word

*Fill in the blanks with words from below.*

1. Jonah said, "Pick me up and throw me into the
_____."

2. A great _____ swallowed Jonah.

3. Jonah prayed, "In my distress I called to the
_____."

4. The Lord told Jonah to go to the city of
_____.

5. The people of Nineveh were _____.

6. The people of Nineveh would be overturned in
_____ days.

7. The Ninevites declared a _____.

8. The Ninevites put on _____.

| | | |
|---|---|---|
| fast | sackcloth | wicked |
| fish | sea | 40 |
| 30 | LORD | Nineveh |

*Draw a line under the word that makes each sentence true.*

1. Jonah was the son of (David—Micah—Amittai—Joshua).

2. The great city of Nineveh was (good—wicked—new—poor).

3. The Lord sent a (wind—rainbow—boat—sailor) on the sea.

4. When Jonah was thrown overboard, the sea grew (choppy—calm—rough—deep).

5. God had (vengeance—pity—compassion—mercy) on the people in the city.

### Applying God's Word

1. By sending Jonah to Nineveh, how did God demonstrate His desire to save all people? _____
_____
_____
_____

2. How is God's salvation for the people of Nineveh like the salvation He offers to us? _____
_____
_____
_____
_____
_____

3. In what way are the story of Jonah and the story of Jesus the same? _____
_____
_____
_____

## 48 Jeremiah

### (Jeremiah 37–38)

## Thinking about God's Word

1. What did Jeremiah tell the king of Judah? _____
_____
_____
_____
_____
_____

2. What did the officials say to the king? _____
_____
_____
_____
_____
_____
_____
_____

3. Where did the officials put Jeremiah? _____
_____

4. What did Ebed-Melech say to the king? _____
_____
_____
_____
_____
_____
_____
_____

5. How did they save him? _____
_____
_____
_____
_____
_____

## Working with God's Word

*Fill in each blank with one word.*

1. According to God's Word to Jeremiah, this ally of Judah would return home instead of coming to Judah's aid. _____

2. _____ was king of Judah.

3. God told Jeremiah that _____ would attack and burn down the city.

4. Lowered into the cistern, Jeremiah sank into the _____.

5. The king commanded his official to take _____ men with him and lift Jeremiah out of the cistern.

*Put a line through the sentences that are not true.*

1. Jeremiah was a prophet.

2. Jeremiah was to tell the king, "Pharaoh's army . . . will go back to its own land, to Egypt."

3. The Amorites were going to return to attack the city.

4. Jeremiah spoke to King Hezekiah.

5. They put Jeremiah into a stream.

## Applying God's Word

1. Why was Jeremiah's message unpopular? When is God's Word unpopular today? _____
_____
_____
_____
_____

2. In what way did God bless Jeremiah through Ebed-Melech? _____
_____
_____
_____

3. How is Jeremiah's release from the cistern similar to Jesus' release from the tomb? How is it different? _____
_____
_____
_____
_____
_____
_____
_____

# 49 The Three Men in the Fiery Furnace
## (Daniel 3)

## Thinking about God's Word

1. How did Nebuchadnezzar sin against the First Commandment? _____ _____ _____ Whom did he gather to come to the dedication? _____ _____

2. How did the king force the people to commit idolatry? _____ _____ _____ How did he threaten to punish them if they disobeyed? _____ _____ _____

3. Who did not obey the command of the king? _____ _____

4. What did the king say to the three men? _____ _____ _____ _____ _____ _____ What did they answer? _____ _____ _____ _____ _____ _____ _____

5. Were the three men sure that God _____ save them? _____ Give a reason. _____ _____ Did the three men know whether or not God _____ to save them? _____ Give a reason. _____ _____ _____ _____

6. Why was Nebuchadnezzar astonished when he looked into the furnace? _____ _____ What did he say? _____ _____

_____
_____
_____
_____
_____
_____

7. What words show that the men were not hurt? _____ _____ _____ _____

8. How did the king now confess that the Lord was stronger than he? _____ _____ _____ _____ _____ _____

## Working with God's Word

*Answer each question on the blank lines.*

1. What did King Nebuchadnezzar have made of gold? _____

2. Why did he have the image made? _____ _____

3. How were those who did not worship the image to be punished? _____ _____

4. Why did the king have the furnace made seven times hotter? _____ _____

5. What was done with the three men before they were thrown into the furnace? _____ _____

6. Who was the fourth man in the furnace? _____ _____

7. Why do you think he had gone into the flames? _____ _____

*Draw a line under the correct answer to each question.*

1. Of what was the idol made?
   (silver—gold—brass—iron)

2. What gave the signal for worshiping the idol?
   (whistle—music—cornet—light)

3. To which people did the three men belong?
   (Chaldeans—Syrians—Jews—Babylonians)

4. How many were thrown into the furnace?
   (1—2—3—4)

5. How many times hotter did the king order the
   furnace made?
   (7—6—2—9)

6. How many people did the king see in the furnace? (1—2—3—4)

7. In which Book of the Bible is this lesson written?
   (1 Kings—2 Kings—3 Samuel—Daniel)

## Applying God's Word

1. Which words show the strong faith of Shadrach,
   Meshach, and Abednego? _____
   _____
   _____
   _____
   _____
   _____
   _____

2. Which character in the account may have been
   Jesus? Describe the Christlike quality of this
   character's actions. _____
   _____
   _____
   _____
   _____

3. Why would Shadrach, Meshach, and Abednego
   still love and thank God even if He would not
   have rescued them from the furnace? _____
   _____
   _____
   _____

# 50 Daniel in the Lions' Den
## (Daniel 6)

### Thinking about God's Word

1. Who was jealous of Daniel? _____
_____ Why
did they want him out of the way? _____
_____
_____

2. Why could the princes find no grounds for
charges against Daniel? _____
_____ How did they
believe they could trap him? _____
_____
_____

3. What edict did they persuade the king to sign?
_____
_____
_____

4. To whom did Daniel always pray? _____
_____ How was that against the king's
decree? _____
_____

5. Who reported Daniel's worship to the king? _____
_____
_____

6. How can you tell that the king thought highly of
Daniel? _____
_____
_____
_____ Which words of the king show that
Daniel must have told Darius about the God of
Israel? _____
_____

7. How did Daniel say that God had protected him?
_____
_____

### Working with God's Word

*Answer each question with one word or a short phrase.*
1. Which king set three administrators over his
kingdom? _____
2. Why could the administrators find no fault in
Daniel? _____
_____

3. Who saved Daniel from the mouths of the lions?
_____

4. Who was glad when he saw that Daniel was safe?
_____

5. To whom did Darius now want the people to
pray? _____

*Draw a line under the answer that makes each sentence
true.*
1. The king made Daniel (a ruler—a king—
a prince—an administrator) in the land.

2. No man was to pray to anyone except (God—
the king—Daniel—the princes).

3. This law was to last for (10—3—20—30) days.

4. The king signed (an edict—a book—a petition—
a dominion).

5. Daniel prayed (10—3—20—30) times a day.

6. Daniel was thrown into a (den—fiery furnace—
prison—pit).

7. The king let Daniel be thrown to the lions
because he (hated Daniel—could not change the
law—wished to please the princes—wanted
Daniel killed).

### Applying God's Word

1. How did the desire to kill Daniel bring death
upon the administrators? _____
_____
_____

2. How did Darius now honor the God of Daniel?
_____
_____
_____
_____

3. What quality of God do the words of King Darius
reveal? _____
_____

# 51 A Message for Zechariah
## (Luke 1)

## Thinking about God's Word

1. Why was Gabriel sent to tell Zechariah about a son? _____
_____

2. Which words show that Gabriel came from God in answer to Zechariah's prayer? _____
_____

3. Why did Zechariah ask, "How can I be sure of this?" _____
_____

4. Who is "the Lord" whom John went before? _____

5. Name one other Bible woman who was blessed with a child only after she had become very old. _____

## Working with God's Word

*Answer each question.*

1. What great event was drawing near at the time of this lesson? _____
_____

2. Which words tell that Zechariah and Elizabeth were God-fearing? _____
_____

3. Which Bible words tell that the couple was very old? _____
_____

4. Why was this old couple not completely happy? _____

5. What good news did an angel bring from God to Zechariah? _____
_____

6. Which words tell what great work John was to perform? _____
_____

7. What happened to Zechariah because he doubted the promise? _____
_____

*Answer each question correctly with one word from below.*

1. Who was Zechariah's wife? _____

2. In which building was Zechariah burning incense? _____

3. What was Zechariah's child to be named? _____

4. Like which great prophet was the child to be? _____

5. For whom was the child to prepare a way? _____

| | | |
|---|---|---|
| Gabriel | temple | Elizabeth |
| Jesus | Elijah | John |
| Mary | Michael | Moses |

## Applying God's Word

1. What is a messenger? _____ _____Why is John a messenger for Jesus? _____
_____

2. The angel came to bring Zechariah good news. How does the angel's message relate to the greatest Good News of all? _____
_____
_____

3. Why is it sometimes hard for us to believe what God says? _____
_____

# 52 The Announcement to Mary
## (Luke 1; Matthew 1)

## Thinking about God's Word

1. Why was Mary afraid of the angel at first? _____
   _____
   _____

2. With which words did Mary say that she was a servant of God? _____
   _____

3. Which words show that God, not Joseph, was to be the true Father of Jesus? _____
   _____
   _____

4. What was the Savior to be named, according to the angel's words? _____ Find three other names for Jesus from this lesson. _____
   _____

## Working with God's Word

*Answer each question.*

1. What words did Gabriel use to greet Mary?
   _____
   _____

2. What was the good news the angel brought to Mary? _____
   
3. In which words did Mary say that she could not understand it all? _____
   _____

4. In which words did the angel say that God can do everything? _____
   _____

5. How did Mary show that she believed the angel's words? _____
   _____
   _____

6. How did Joseph learn of God's wonderful promise? _____

7. How did Joseph show that he believed God's promise? _____
   _____

*By drawing a line from word to word, match the words given below with their meanings.*

| Word | Meaning |
| --- | --- |
| pledged | rule |
| virgin | thought about |
| favored | greatly honored |
| wondered | promised |
| reign | woman who has not had sexual intercourse |

## Applying God's Word

1. Which words of the lesson show that the Savior was to be true man, born of a woman? _____
   _____

   What was to be His work? _____
   _____

2. Which words of the Apostles' Creed are clearly referenced in Gabriel's message to Mary? _____
   _____

3. Why was it necessary for the world's Savior to be a human? _____
   _____

# 53 The Birth of John the Baptist

## (Luke 1)

## Thinking about God's Word

1. How did God's promise to Zechariah and Elizabeth come true? _____

2. Which words show that Elizabeth's neighbors and cousins knew that the child came from God? _____ _____ _____

3. In the naming of their son, how did the parents show that they had learned to obey and trust God without question? _____ _____

4. How did Zechariah use his loosed tongue, which once had spoken words of doubt at God's promise? _____

## Working with God's Word

*Answer each question.*

1. How were the angel's words fulfilled? _____ _____ _____

2. What did the parents do eight days after John was born? _____

3. How did Zechariah settle the matter of naming the child? _____ _____

4. What did Zechariah prophesy about his son? ___ _____ _____ _____ _____ _____ _____

5. Where was John until the day he appeared to Israel? _____

*Answer each question with one word from below.*

1. On which day was the baby circumcised? _____

2. What did the neighbors want to name the baby? _____

3. What did the mother name him? _____

4. What did the father name him? _____

5. For whom was this child to prepare the way? _____

6. Who asked for a writing tablet? _____

7. What special ability did the Holy Spirit give Zechariah to do? _____

| | | | |
|---|---|---|---|
| Zechariah | eighth | Paul | baptize |
| prophesy | Jesus | John | fifth |

## Applying God's Word

1. Which words, prophesied by Zechariah, refer to the work of Jesus, our Savior? _____ _____ _____

2. When our wisdom and learning advise us to do the opposite of what God wants, to whom must we listen? _____ Why? _____ _____

3. How can you show your thankfulness to God for having kept His promises? _____ _____

# 54 The Birth of Jesus
## (Luke 2)

## Thinking about God's Word

1. Name three prophecies about the Savior's coming made by Old Testament prophets. _____
_____
_____

2. Who was Caesar Augustus? _____
_____

3. How did God use Caesar Augustus to bring Mary and Joseph to the place where Jesus was to be born? _____
_____
_____

4. Which simple words tell how the Savior of the world was born at Bethlehem? _____
_____
_____
_____
_____
_____
_____

5. What difference would it make to us if Jesus had not been born? _____
_____
_____

6. How do you know that Jesus was born? _____
_____

7. Who gave the Christ Child to us as a gift of love? Find the answer in John 3:16. _____

## Working with God's Word

*Answer each question.*

1. What great time in the world's history now had come? _____

2. What new law did the Roman emperor make for the Roman world? _____
_____

3. Who had chosen this time to fulfill His promises? _____

4. Where was each person to go to be taxed?
_____

5. What was the name of the town to which Joseph and Mary went? _____

6. To whose family did Mary and Joseph belong? _____

7. What great happiness came to Mary in Bethlehem? _____

8. In what did Mary wrap her baby? _____

9. Who was this Child? _____

*Draw a line under the word that makes each sentence true.*

1. The emperor made a law that all (Romans—Jews—the world) should be taxed.

2. (Caesar Augustus—Quirinius—Julius) was the governor of Syria when Jesus was born.

3. Everyone had to go to (Rome—Bethlehem—his own city) to be taxed.

4. (Jerusalem—Nazareth—Bethlehem) was the city of David.

5. Mary laid her baby (in a cradle—on the ground— in a manger).

6. Mary and Joseph had come from (Syria—Jerusalem—Nazareth) to be taxed.

7. (David—Joseph—God) was the true Father of the Child Jesus.

## Applying God's Word

1. Describe the circumstances surrounding the birth of the Son of God. What is unusual about the surroundings into which He was born? _____
_____
_____
_____
_____

2. Of what should the giving of presents at Christmas remind Christians? _____
_____

3. Why is the birth of Jesus such a significant event?
_____
_____

## 55 Angels Announce the Savior's Birth
### (Luke 2)

### Thinking about God's Word

1. What kind of birth announcement did God send when Jesus was born? _____
_____

2. How did God show that He wanted the good news of His Son's birth to be known by the common, ordinary people? _____
_____

3. What was good about the news that the angel brought? _____

4. Which words show that the good news was meant for all the people in the world? _____
_____

5. What song of praise did the angels sing to God for His goodness? _____
_____
_____

6. What did the shepherds do after they had heard and seen the angels? _____
_____

7. Which words show that Mary, the mother of Jesus, remembered all these events? _____
_____
_____

### Working with God's Word

*On the blank lines write a few words from the Bible story that answer the following questions.*

1. Where were the shepherds? _____
_____

2. When did the angel appear? _____

3. What shone around the shepherd? _____
_____

4. Who had been born this day? _____

5. Where did the angels come from? _____

6. How do you know the shepherds believed the angel? _____
_____

7. Where did the shepherds find the baby lying?
_____

*Fill in the blanks with words from below.*

1. The shepherds were watching over their _____ during the night.

2. When the angel appeared, the shepherds were _____.

3. The angel called the newborn child a _____.

4. A great company of the heavenly _____ sang a song of praise.

5. The shepherds spread the _____ about Jesus.

6. Mary treasured up all these things and _____ them in her heart.

7. The shepherds could be called the first _____.

| | | | |
|---|---|---|---|
| missionaries | host | flocks | pondered |
| Joseph | word | Savior | terrified |
| Bethlehem | | | |

### Applying God's Word

1. Why is the birth of Jesus one of the all-time great events of human history? _____
_____
_____

2. What is the peace that Jesus would bring? _____
_____
_____
_____

3. Who told you the good news of how Jesus was born for you? _____
How can you show your thankfulness for having been told these wonderful things? _____
_____
_____

# 56 The Presentation of Jesus
## (Luke 2)

## Thinking about God's Word

1. How did Jesus' parents keep the Law of Moses for Him when He was eight days old? _____

   _____

   Which law did they obey when He was 40 days old? _____

   _____

   _____

2. What name was given to the Savior at the time of His circumcision? _____ What is the meaning of that name? _____

3. What words describing Simeon show him to be a man of faith? _____

   _____

## Working with God's Word

*Answer each question.*

1. Where did Jesus' parents go to present Him to the Lord? _____

2. Who was waiting for the Savior's coming in Jerusalem? _____

3. What special promise had been given Simeon by the Holy Spirit? _____

   _____

4. Why was Simeon in the temple on this day?

   _____

   _____

5. In which words did Simeon say that the Lord had kept His promise? _____

   _____

6. Which of Simeon's words say that Jesus is the Savior of all people? _____

   _____

   _____

7. Who marveled at the words of Simeon? _____

   _____

*Draw a line under the word or phrase that makes each sentence true.*

1. Jesus was (born—circumcised—promised) on the eighth day.

2. Jesus was presented at the temple (in Nazareth—in Jerusalem—in Bethlehem).

3. The Holy Spirit had told Simeon that before his death he would (become very old—preach in the temple—see the Savior).

4. Simeon was (late and old—righteous and devout—very sad).

5. Simeon said that Jesus was (a great king—not a heathen—salvation).

## Applying God's Word

1. Who is meant by the "salvation" of which Simeon spoke? _____ How is Jesus your salvation?

   _____

   _____

2. Why was Simeon ready to die after having seen Jesus? _____

   _____

3. Why can you die without fear, just as Simeon was able to do? _____

   _____

# 57 The Magi from the East
## (Matthew 2)

## Thinking about God's Word

1. Who were the people from the East who came to see Jesus? _____

2. What led them from their land to the Holy Land? _____ Why did they need a star to guide them? _____

_____

3. How did the chief priests and scribes of Jesus' time discover where the Savior was to be born? See Micah 5:2 in your Bible. _____

_____

4. Who said to the Magi, "Go and make a careful search for the child"? _____

5. Why did Herod ask the Magi to let him know where Jesus was to be found? _____

_____ Why did God warn the Magi not to tell Herod where Jesus was? _____

_____

## Working with God's Word

*Answer each question.*

1. What are the Magi also called? _____

2. Why was Herod disturbed at the words of the Magi? _____

3. From whom did Herod learn where Jesus was to be born? _____

_____

4. What answer was given Herod when he wished to know Jesus' birthplace? _____

_____

5. How did the Magi show that they believed Jesus to be God? _____

_____

*Answer each question with words from below.*

1. From where did the Wise Men come? _____

2. At which city did they stop for information?

_____

3. What did the Wise Men call Jesus? _____

_____

4. Who was troubled about the Wise Men's question? _____

5. What led the Wise Men from the East? _____

6. Whom did the Wise Men find with the Child?

_____

7. How did God warn the Magi not to see Herod?

_____

| Mary | aloes | Jerusalem |
|------|-------|-----------|
| Nazareth | East | by an angel |
| by a dream | Herod | King of the Jews |
| Persia | star | |

## Applying God's Word

1. What did Herod not understand about Jesus' kingship? See Jesus' words to Pilate in John 18:33–37. _____

_____

_____

_____

2. How were the words of Simeon being fulfilled at the coming of the Magi? See Luke 2:32.

_____

_____

_____

_____

3. What action on the part of the Magi suggests that they believed in Jesus as the Savior (Matthew 2:11)? _____

_____

_____

# 58 The Escape to Egypt
## (Matthew 2)

## Thinking about God's Word

1. Jeremiah prophesied the "Slaughter of the Innocents," which took place at this time. In what respect were the boys in Bethlehem innocent?

   _____

   _____

2. How might one of the gifts that the Magi brought to Jesus have been put to good use at this time?

   _____

   _____

3. Why should God's children be happy to know that the angels are always near them? _____

   _____

   _____ How did God use angels in this story?

   _____

   _____

4. Name other Bible people who lived in Egypt.

   _____

   _____

   _____

5. By whom were the ancestors of Jesus led out of Egypt? _____

## Working with God's Word

*Fill in the blanks.*

1. The angel of the Lord appeared to _____ in a dream.

2. Herod was seeking the young Child to _____ Him.

3. Joseph traveled with the young Child and the mother during the _____.

4. Herod killed boys _____ years old and under.

5. An angel of the Lord appeared in a dream to Joseph in _____.

6. Joseph was told to take Mary and Jesus back to the land of _____.

7. They returned and lived in a city called _____.

## Applying God's Word

1. What details of this account show Joseph to be a man of faith? How do others come to know about your faith in Jesus? _____

   _____

   _____

   _____

   _____

2. What does it mean to you to know that God kept all His promises and prophecies in Jesus? _____

   _____

3. How did God defend Jesus against all danger and guard and protect Him from all evil? _____

   _____

   _____ How does God do the same for you daily? _____

   _____

## 59 The Boy Jesus at the Temple
### (Luke 2)

### Thinking about God's Word

1. When Jesus was 12 years old, where did His parents take Him? _____

2. Which words tell that Jesus' parents were faithful worshipers at the temple? _____ _____

3. Where did Jesus say He had been while His parents looked for Him? _____ _____

4. Read Colossians 2:3. How did the teachers in the temple find the words to be true? _____ _____ _____

5. Why did Jesus study Scripture even though "all the treasures of wisdom and knowledge" are to be found in Him? _____ _____ _____

6. Which words tell that Mary and Joseph were very worried over the thought of losing Jesus? _____ _____ _____

7. What reason did Jesus give for staying behind in Jerusalem? _____ _____

### Working with God's Word

*Answer each question.*

1. What great festival did Jesus' parents attend each year? _____

2. Where was this festival held? _____

3. Why did the parents not worry over Jesus' absence on the return trip? _____ _____ _____

4. How long did Joseph and Mary look for Jesus before finding Him? _____

5. What was it about Jesus that amazed all who heard Him? _____ _____

6. In which words did Jesus answer the question His mother asked Him? _____ _____

7. What was His Father's house? _____

*On the blank lines write the word from below that you think of as you read each sentence.*

1. It lasted seven days. _____

2. Jesus was sitting in the midst of them. _____

3. Where they found Jesus. _____

4. Jesus had to be about His business. _____

5. Mary, Joseph, and Jesus returned there to live. _____

6. Here it was that Mary kept all Jesus' sayings. _____

7. Jesus kept this commandment when He obeyed His parents. _____

| | | |
|---|---|---|
| temple | fourth | heart |
| Passover | first | teachers |
| Nazareth | His Father's | |

### Applying God's Word

1. What details of this account show Jesus to be true God? What details of this account show Jesus to be truly human? _____ _____ _____ _____

2. What has been offered to you to help you in learning and knowing Scripture? Name people and things that have helped you. _____ _____

3. Two commandments of God were clearly obeyed by Jesus in this lesson. What are they? How did Jesus obey them? How can you follow His example? _____ _____ _____ _____ _____ _____

# 60 The Baptism of Jesus
## (Matthew 3; Mark 1)

## Thinking about God's Word

1. Who came to John to be baptized? _____

2. How can you tell that John recognized Jesus as the Christ? _____
   _____
   _____

3. What was the theme of the message John preached? _____

4. How did God show Jesus as the Savior whom He had promised to send? _____
   _____
   _____

5. What prophet foretold the ministry of John the Baptist? _____

## Working with God's Word

*Answer each question.*

1. How did John answer Jesus when He asked to be baptized? _____
   _____

2. What reason did Jesus give John for being baptized by him? _____
   _____
   _____

3. How was each person of the Trinity shown at this baptism? _____
   _____
   _____

*On the blank lines write words from below.*

1. He came from Galilee to the Jordan._____

2. He preached in the desert. _____

3. He descended like a dove. _____

4. He said, "I need to be baptized by You." _____

5. He said, "Let it be so now." _____

6. He is the Father's beloved Son. _____

7. Who wrote the first book of the New Testament?
   _____

| | | |
|---|---|---|
| Holy Spirit | God the Father | John |
| Matthew | John the Baptist | Jesus |

## Applying God's Word

1. In what way did John "prepare the way for the Lord"? _____
   _____
   _____

2. In what two ways did the people respond to the preaching of John? _____
   _____
   _____

3. Why did Jesus not need to be baptized as a sign of repentance? _____
   _____
   _____ Why, then, was He baptized? _____
   _____
   _____
   _____

# 61 The Temptation of Jesus
## (Matthew 4)

## Thinking about God's Word

1. Into whose power had man fallen when Adam sinned? _____

2. Why had Jesus come into the world? _____ _____

3. Why did Satan want to keep Jesus from doing His work? _____ _____ How did the devil plan to spoil what Jesus had come to do? _____

4. How did the devil first try to plant the seed of doubt into Jesus, as he once had done to Adam and Eve? _____ _____

5. When Satan tempted Jesus the second time, how did he try to twist God's Word to lead Jesus into sin? _____ _____ _____ _____ _____ How had he twisted God's Word in the Garden of Eden? _____ _____ _____ _____

6. In the third temptation, how did the devil use humankind's love for honor and possessions to try to lead the Savior into sin? _____ _____ _____ _____ _____ How had he used the same kind of temptation against Adam and Eve? _____ _____ _____

7. Which words spoken three times show that Jesus knew Scripture and used it correctly against the devil? _____

## Working with God's Word

*Answer each question.*

1. Where was Jesus led after His baptism? _____ _____

2. How long did Jesus fast there? _____ _____

3. In which words did the devil first tempt Jesus to sin? _____ _____

4. According to Jesus' words, by what shall man really live? _____ _____

5. Where did the devil take Jesus for the second temptation? _____ _____

6. How did the devil tempt Jesus there? _____ _____ _____ _____ _____ _____ _____

7. In which words did Jesus answer this temptation? _____ _____

8. What did the devil say in tempting Jesus the third time? _____ _____

9. What was Jesus' final answer to the devil's temptations? _____ _____ _____

*Fill in the blanks with words from below.*

1. Jesus said, "Away from Me, _____.

2. The devil asked Jesus to turn _____ to bread.

3. The devil showed Jesus all the _____ of the world.

4. Angels came and _____ Jesus.

5. Jesus was led into the wilderness by the _____.

6. The devil asked Jesus to fall down and _____ him.

7. Jesus said, "Do not put the _____ your God to the test."

8. The devil had Jesus stand on the _____ point of the temple.

9. Three times Jesus said, "It is _____."

| | | | |
|---|---|---|---|
| written | kingdoms | Satan | worship |
| attended | Lord | Spirit | highest |
| stones | | | |

## Applying God's Word

1. What was the difference in outcome between Satan's attempt to lead Adam into sin and his attempt to lead Jesus into sin? _____

   _____

   _____

2. This account shows how Jesus obeyed God's Law in our place. Explain. _____

   _____

   _____

   _____

3. In facing and resisting temptation, Jesus pointed us to the means through which the Holy Spirit strengthens us to resist temptations. What is that means? _____

   _____

   _____

   _____

   _____

   _____

## 62 Jesus Helps Peter Catch Fish
### (Luke 5)

### Thinking about God's Word

1. Show that the people in this story were eager to hear God's Word. _____
_____

2. What do you think Jesus talked about to the people? _____
_____

3. Why did Simon not seem to think it wise to go fishing again? _____
_____ What was it that made him willing to let down the net, nevertheless? _____

4. Which words show that the nets had not been made to hold so great a number of fish? _____

5. Which words show that the two boats together had not been built large enough to hold the catch of fish that Jesus gave them? _____
_____

6. How did Peter show that he knew he had seen a miracle? _____
_____
_____

7. Which words say that these disciples now gave their whole life to become followers and disciples of Jesus? _____
_____
_____

### Working with God's Word

*Answer each question on the blank line.*

1. Why do you think Jesus got on a boat to teach the people? _____
_____

2. Whose ship did Jesus use? _____

3. What was Jesus' command to Simon after He had finished speaking? _____
_____
_____

4. Which words tell why Simon was willing to let down the nets? _____

5. Which words tell that many fish were in the net?

_____
_____
_____

6. What did Simon Peter say when he saw all the fish? _____

7. How did these disciples give themselves to Jesus from then on? _____
_____

*Draw a line under the correct answer to each question.*

1. What is another name for the Sea of Galilee? (Red Sea—Salt Sea—Lake of Gennesaret—Dead Sea)

2. How was the water where Jesus told the disciples to fish? (deep—shallow—muddy—warm)

3. How many fish did they catch? (none—1—a few—many)

4. What did Jesus tell Simon Peter that he would catch from now on? (fish—draughts—thieves—men)

5. How many boats were filled with fish? (1—2—3—4—5—6—none—many)

### Applying God's Word

1. Why did Jesus teach and preach? _____
_____ What did He preach about? _____
_____

2. By what action did Peter demonstrate his faith in Jesus? _____
_____
_____
By what words? _____
_____

3. What does the amount of fish in the catch show about the growth expected in God's kingdom? _____
_____
_____
_____
_____

74

# 63 Jesus Changes Water to Wine

## (John 2)

### Thinking about God's Word

1. Why was it not hard for Jesus' followers to believe that He was a true man? _____ _____ _____ _____

2. How did Jesus show Himself to be true God before the people at Cana? _____ _____

3. What did Jesus use to turn water into wine? _____

4. Which words of the lesson tell why He did this miracle? _____ _____ _____

5. Who went to Jesus for help in this lesson? _____ Why should we go to Jesus when we need help? _____ _____

6. No doubt John was present at Cana when Jesus did His first miracle. How did John and the other disciples see the glory of Jesus at Cana? _____ _____

7. How many gallons did each water jar hold? ____ _____ How many jars were there? _____

### Working with God's Word

*Answer the questions.*

1. What trouble brought Mary to Jesus for His help? _____

2. Why were six water jars in the house? _____ _____

3. To whom was some water taken after it had been changed to wine? _____ _____

4. Which words tell where Jesus began doing miracles? _____

5. Which words tell why Jesus did this great miracle? _____ _____ _____

*Fill in the blanks with words from below.*

1. There was a wedding in the city of _____.

2. Mary, Jesus, and His _____ were invited.

3. The people ran out of _____.

4. Jesus said, "My _____ has not yet come."

5. Mary told the _____ to do whatever Jesus might command.

6. There were _____ stone water jars in this home.

7. The servants filled the water jars to the _____.

8. By His power, Jesus turned the _____ into good wine.

| | | |
|---|---|---|
| servants | mother | time |
| six | eight | wine |
| Cana | miracles | brim |
| water | disciples | father |

### Applying God's Word

1. How do we know that Mary had faith in Jesus' power? _____ _____

2. Tell how this account shows Jesus as both true man and true God. _____ _____ _____ _____ _____

3. What does this account indicate about the scope of human problems about which Jesus is concerned? _____ _____ _____ _____

# 64 Jesus Calms the Storm
## (Mark 4)

## Thinking about God's Word

1. How can it be shown from this lesson that Jesus was true man? _____

2. Why did the disciples awaken Jesus?_____
_____
_____

3. Why did they ask Jesus for His help even though they were experienced sailors? _____
_____

4. How did Jesus still the storm? _____
_____

5. Why did the wind and sea obey Jesus? _____
_____

6. Show from this lesson that Jesus was true God-man. _____
_____
_____

7. Who permitted this great storm to come up? _____ Why does God let trials and temptations come to His children? _____
_____
_____

## Working with God's Word

*Circle T for true and F for false.*

1. This lesson says: "It had been a busy day for Jesus." T F

2. This lesson says: "Jesus was tired from a hard day's work." T F

3. This lesson says: "They got into a boat and set out." T F

4. This lesson says: "As they sailed, He fell asleep." T F

5. This lesson says: "A furious squall came up." T F

6. This lesson says: "And His disciples came to Him." T F

7. This lesson says: "Lord, save us!" T F

8. This lesson says: "Why are you so afraid?" T F

9. This lesson says: "He arose and quieted the wind." T F

10. This lesson says: "Then the wind died down and it was completely calm." T F

*Circle Yes or No.*

1. Jesus and His disciples wanted to reach the other side of the lake. Yes No

2. Because Jesus slept, we know that He was true God. Yes No

3. The great storm awakened Jesus. Yes No

4. Jesus asked the disciples why they had no faith. Yes No

5. Jesus said to the sea, "Quiet! Be still!" Yes No

## Applying God's Word

1. Which part of the disciples' cry showed that they were without trust and hope, even while they asked Jesus for help? _____
_____

   Why was this wrong? _____
_____
_____

2. In which words did Jesus tell the disciples what the real reason for all their worry and fear had been? _____
_____
_____

3. Why can we always trust in Jesus? _____
_____

# 65 Jesus Heals a Man Who Was Paralyzed
## (Mark 2)

## Thinking about God's Word

1. Why did the four men bring their sick friend to Jesus? _____ _____ How did they show their faith in His power to help? _____ _____ _____ _____

2. Which words tell what the man needed more than the healing of his body? _____ _____ How could Jesus know this about the man? _____ _____

3. Why did the teachers think that Jesus had mocked God? _____ _____ _____

4. What do we learn from the fact that Jesus could tell their thoughts? _____ _____

5. How did Jesus prove His power? _____ _____

## Working with God's Word

*Answer each question with one word or a short phrase.*

1. What was the sickness that the man of this lesson had? _____

2. To which city did the Lord return? _____

3. How many men carried the sick man? _____

4. What did the men do so the man could reach Jesus? _____ _____

5. What did Jesus call the sick man when He spoke to him? _____

*Draw a line under the word or phrase that makes each sentence true.*

1. Jesus was (outside—inside) when the man was brought to Him.

2. The first thing Jesus did for the man was to (ask his name—heal his sickness—forgive his sins).

3. (Jesus—The sick man—The teachers) said, "Who can forgive sins but God alone?"

4. Jesus called Himself (the Messiah—the Son of Man—the Just One) in this lesson.

5. The teachers spoke evil things of Jesus (to themselves—so that all could hear it—in a low voice).

6. Jesus told the sick man to take up his (blanket—couch—mattress—mat) and go home.

7. The people who saw this miracle (laughed at the scribes—told Jesus to leave their country—glorified God).

## Applying God's Word

1. Describe the kind of friends God provided the man with paralysis. _____ _____ _____

2. Which words of the lesson show why Jesus did miracles openly? _____ _____ _____ _____

3. According to this account, what type of healing provided by Jesus do people need the most? _____

## 66 A Widow's Son and Jairus' Daughter

### (Luke 7–8)

### Thinking about God's Word

1. How did Jesus raise the widow's son to life? ____
   _____
   _____

2. Why was Jairus wise in going to Jesus for help?
   _____
   _____
   _____

3. What did Jesus mean when He said, "The girl is not dead but asleep"? _____
   _____
   _____

4. At what other time did Jesus prove that He had the same power? _____
   _____

5. Why did Jesus' words "Don't cry," as spoken to the widow, have comfort and meaning for her?
   _____

### Working with God's Word

*Answer each question.*

1. What did Jesus meet as He entered Nain one day? _____

2. How did Jesus show His great sorrow for the mother? _____
   _____

3. By which miracle did Jesus comfort the mother?
   _____

4. In which words did the people glorify God upon seeing the miracle? _____
   _____

5. How did Jairus show his faith in Jesus? _____
   _____
   _____
   _____

6. What sad message did someone bring to Jairus?
   _____

7. How did Jesus show the people His power over death? _____
   _____

*Draw a line under the correct answer to each question.*

1. How many sons did the widow have?
   (1—2—3—4—0—5)

2. On what was the young man being carried? (bed—stretcher—coffin—bier)

3. Over what was Jairus a ruler?
   (Palestine—synagogue—Judea—Galilee)

4. How old was his sick daughter?
   (30—12—20—5—6)

5. What did Jesus call death in this lesson? (the end of everything—damnation—sleep—heaven)

6. How did the people in Jairus' house show unbelief in Jesus? (cast Him out—laughed at Him—left the room—closed their ears)

7. What was given Jairus' daughter after Jesus brought her to life? (food—wine—water—rest)

### Applying God's Word

1. How did Jesus show the people of Jairus' city His power over death? _____
   _____

2. Because of Jesus, the death of Jairus' daughter and of the widow's son really was just a short sleep that had a happy ending. Why does death mean the same thing for you too? _____
   _____
   _____

3. Responding to the restoration of the young man of Nain, the people said, "God has come to help His people." Describe the help Jesus came to provide. _____
   _____
   _____
   _____

# 67 Jesus Feeds More Than Five Thousand
## (John 6)

## Thinking about God's Word

1. What did Jesus ask Philip? _____

_____

_____ How did Philip's answer show that he thought money was of first importance in getting food for hungry people? _____

_____

_____

_____

2. Why was Andrew's answer a hopeless response to Jesus' question? _____

_____

_____

3. In which prayer do we say, "Give us this day our daily bread"? _____

Why do we ask for it even when we know we'll get it? _____

_____

_____

## Working with God's Word

*Fill in the blanks.*

1. A great _____ followed Jesus.

2. Jesus went up on a _____.

3. When Jesus looked up, He saw a great _____.

4. Jesus said to _____, "Where shall we buy bread?"

5. _____ found the boy with loaves and fishes.

6. Before Jesus gave out food, He _____ God.

7. He distributed to the people as much food as they _____.

8. Twelve baskets were filled with the _____ that remained.

9. The people saw that Jesus had done a _____.

*Mark the true sentences T and the false sentences F.*

1. ___ Jesus crossed to the far side of the Sea of Galilee.

2. ___ Jesus asked Andrew, "Where shall we buy bread?"

3. ___ Philip said that eight months' wages would not be enough.

4. ___ Andrew found a boy who had a little food with him.

5. ___ The boy had two fishes and five barley loaves.

6. ___ Jesus gave each of the five thousand a loaf and a fish.

7. ___ The people ate as much as they wanted.

## Applying God's Word

1. Jesus' miracles led the people to see Jesus as a great prophet. Jesus is more than a prophet. Explain.

_____

_____

2. Which words of the lesson show that Jesus gave the people more than they wanted and needed?

_____

_____ Why could He do this? _____

_____

3. Jesus could have simply taken away the people's hunger. Instead, He satisfied their hunger by multiplying a meager lunch of bread and fish. In another meal, the Lord's Supper, Jesus also provides for His followers. What do they receive with the bread and wine? _____

_____

_____

What benefits are received? _____

_____

_____

# 68   Jesus Walks on the Water
## (Mark 6; Matthew 14)

## Thinking about God's Word

1. What did the multitude whom Jesus fed want to do to Him? _____

2. How did the disciples obey Jesus' command? _____ _____ How was their faith tested that night? _____ _____ _____

3. How did they show that they didn't believe that it was Jesus when they saw Him coming toward them? _____

4. What did Jesus say to them? _____ _____ How did those words show why He had come to them? _____ _____ _____

5. Why could Jesus walk on water? _____ _____ Why could Peter walk on water? _____ _____

6. What did Peter cry out when he began to sink? _____ _____

7. Which words of Jesus tell why Peter began to sink? _____ How did Jesus show Peter that He was the merciful Son of God? _____ _____

## Working with God's Word

*Answer each question with one word from the story.*

1. Whom did Jesus send away? _____
2. Who went before Him to Bethsaida? _____
3. During which watch did Jesus come to His disciples? _____
4. What did the disciples think Jesus was when they saw Him? _____
5. With which word did Jesus tell Peter to come to Him? _____

6. How did Peter become when he saw the wind blowing? _____
7. What died down when Jesus stepped into the boat? _____

*Draw a line under the correct answer to each question.*

1. Whom did the people want for their king? (Herod—Tabors—Jesus—Philip)
2. Why did Jesus go up on a mountainside? (to preach—to pray—to hide—to rest)
3. Where was the boat when a storm arose? (a distance from land—on the other side— along the coast)
4. How did Jesus cross the sea to get to the disciples? (by rowing—by sailing—by swimming— by walking)
5. What happened when Jesus climbed into the boat? (The disciples cried—The disciples rowed to shore—The wind died down)

## Applying God's Word

1. Jesus spoke to His disciples in their fear, saying, "Take courage! It is I. Don't be afraid." How do these words of Jesus apply also to us? _____ _____ _____

2. What happened when Peter trusted in Jesus? What happened when he doubted? _____ _____ _____ _____

3. What realization led the disciples to worship Jesus? _____ _____ _____

# 69 The Faith of a Canaanite Woman
## (Matthew 15)

## Thinking about God's Word

1. What made it seem that Jesus did not care to help the Canaanite woman? _____ _____ _____ _____

2. For what reason did the disciples ask Jesus to send her away? _____ _____ _____

3. Why did Jesus say that the woman had no right to ask for His help? _____ _____

4. In which words did the woman answer Jesus when He said that helping her would be like throwing children's bread to dogs? _____ _____ _____

5. In which words did Jesus say why He would answer the woman's prayer? _____ _____ _____

## Working with God's Word

*Answer each question.*

1. Who came to Jesus for help? _____ _____

2. With which words did the woman tell what was wrong with her daughter? _____ _____ _____

3. Who said, "Send her away, for she keeps crying out after us"? _____

4. Which words say that Jesus came for the Jews first? _____ _____

5. With which words did the woman worship Jesus? _____ _____

6. In which words did Jesus praise this woman's faith? _____ _____

7. How did Jesus answer the faithful prayer of this woman? _____

*Draw a line under the answer that makes each sentence true.*

1. The woman who came to Jesus was a (Jew—Roman—Greek—Galilean—Babylonian).

2. The woman asked for (bread—mercy—meat—alms—great riches).

3. At first Jesus answered the woman (not a word—"Go to a doctor"—"Depart from Me"—very kindly).

4. Jesus told the woman that her (daughter's sickness—sin—faith—age) was great.

5. Her daughter was healed from that (year—day—hour).

## Applying God's Word

1. Which words of the woman showed that she knew Jesus to be the promised Savior? _____ _____

2. Which words show that the woman knew she didn't deserve the help she was asking of Him? _____ _____ _____

3. In what way is each of us like the woman in the lesson? What does the lesson teach us about Jesus? _____ _____ _____ _____

# 70 The Ten Lepers

### (Luke 17)

## Thinking about God's Word

1. Where was Jesus going? _____

2. Why did the men want Jesus to have pity on them? _____

3. Who came back to praise God? _____
   _____

4. What did Jesus mean when He said, "Where are the other nine?" _____
   _____
   _____

5. Why was the leper healed? _____
   _____

## Working with God's Word

*Fill in the blank with a word from the story.*

1. Jesus traveled along the border between _____ and Galilee.

2. _____ men with leprosy met Him.

3. They called, "Jesus, _____, have pity on us!"

4. Jesus told them to show themselves to the _____.

5. One of the men came back and _____ God in a loud voice.

6. Jesus asked, "Were not all ten _____?"

7. "Where are the other _____?"

8. Jesus said to the Samaritan, "_____ and go; your faith has made you well."

*Write who made these statements. Use the words* Jesus *or* 10 men.

1. "Were not all ten cleansed?" _____

2. "Rise and go; your faith has made you well." _____

3. "Jesus, Master, have pity on us." _____

4. "Was no one found to return and give praise to God except this foreigner?" _____

5. "Where are the other nine?" _____

6. "Go, show yourselves to the priests." _____

## Applying God's Word

1. Why did Jesus want the men to see the priests?
   _____
   _____
   _____

2. Tell how this account shows Jesus as the Lord and Savior of all people. _____
   _____
   _____
   _____
   _____

3. What example does the Samaritan provide for all of us who love and trust in Jesus as our Savior?
   _____
   _____
   _____
   _____
   _____

# 71 Jesus Blesses the Children
## (Matthew 18–19)

## Thinking about God's Word

1. What did the disciples ask Jesus? _____
_____

2. With which direct words did Jesus tell them that if they didn't change, they wouldn't get into the kingdom of heaven? _____
_____
_____
_____

3. How did Jesus warn the disciples that they were not to look lightly upon the child who stood in their midst nor to offend such a little believer?
_____
_____
_____
_____
_____
_____

4. In which words did Jesus tell the disciples that they were to lead little children to Him rather than to keep them away? _____
_____
_____
_____

5. Who did Jesus say is the greatest in His kingdom?
_____
_____

## Working with God's Word

*Answer each question.*

1. To whom is Jesus a particular friend? _____
2. Whom did Jesus call the greatest in the kingdom of heaven? _____
_____
3. Whom do people welcome when they welcome a child in Jesus' name? _____
4. Which words tell that the disciples scolded those who brought them? _____
_____
5. In which words did Jesus say that He wanted children to come to Him? _____
_____

*Draw a line under the correct answer to each question.*

1. Who came to Jesus to ask Him a question? (parents—disciples—children—scribes)

2. What did they want to know? (Who Jesus' best friend was—If He loved children—Who would be greatest in the kingdom of heaven)

3. How can a person become as a little child? (by not studying too much—by trusting altogether in Jesus—by not sinning)

4. When is a child not a child of God? (when the child does not go to church every Sunday—when the child becomes older—when the child does not believe)

5. Why were the children brought to Jesus? (for Him to heal them—for Him to teach them—for Him to pray for them)

6. How did Jesus feel when He saw what the disciples did? (He wept—He was not pleased—He was pleased)

7. How did Jesus show His love for the little ones? (He gave them presents—He kissed them—He preached to them—He blessed them)

## Applying God's Word

1. Why must little children simply trust their parents for everything they need? _____
_____ With which words did Jesus tell the disciples that in order to be in His kingdom they must be toward Him as little children are toward parents? _____
_____
_____
_____

2. According to this account, how does God in heaven protect little children? _____
_____

3. How do people "change and become like little children" in order to enter the kingdom of heaven? _____
_____
_____

# 72 The Transfiguration
## (Matthew 17)

## Thinking about God's Word

1. What did Jesus look like in His transfiguration?
   _____
   _____
   _____

2. Who appeared with Jesus? _____
   _____

3. Which disciples went with Jesus up the mountain? _____

4. What did Peter want to do for Jesus? _____
   _____
   _____
   _____

5. What did the voice from the cloud say? _____
   _____
   _____

6. Why were the disciples afraid? _____
   _____

7. Why did Jesus tell them not to tell anyone what they had seen? _____
   _____
   _____

## Working with God's Word

*Write T for true or F for false.*

1. Jesus took Peter, James, and Matthew with Him to the mountain. _____

2. Jesus was transfigured on the mountain. _____

3. Elijah and Isaiah appeared, talking with Jesus.
   _____

4. The men were talking about Jesus' departure.
   _____

5. The disciples were sleepy. _____

6. Peter offered to build three shelters. _____

7. God's voice came from a fire. _____

8. The disciples were terrified of the voice.
   _____

*Fill in the blanks with words from below.*

After _____ days Jesus took _____, _____, and John up a mountain. He was _____ before them. Two men, _____ and _____, appeared with Jesus. Peter offered to build _____ _____ for the three. A voice came from a _____ saying Jesus was God's _____. _____ told the disciples not to tell what they had seen.

| | | |
|---|---|---|
| Moses | two | Peter |
| cloud | Jesus | six |
| John | transfigured | Elijah |
| Son | James | shelters |

## Applying God's Word

1. What theme from the life and teaching of the prophets was fulfilled in Christ? _____
   _____
   _____

2. What event, about to take place in Jerusalem, became the subject of those talking with Jesus at His transfiguration? _____
   _____
   _____ Why was this topic significant? _____
   _____
   _____

3. Tell the meaning of the words spoken from the bright cloud for the disciples and for you. _____
   _____
   _____
   _____
   _____
   _____
   _____
   _____

# 73  Zacchaeus

**(Luke 19)**

## Thinking about God's Word

1. Why didn't Zacchaeus go home when he couldn't see Jesus because of the crowd? _____

_____

2. How do we know that Jesus was looking for Zacchaeus when He came to the tree? _____

_____

_____

3. Why did some people mutter? _____

_____

4. Was Jesus the guest of a sinner? Explain your answer. _____

_____

Why did He go with Zacchaeus? _____

_____

_____

5. Show how Zacchaeus's life was changed after he was found by Jesus and received Him as his Savior. _____

_____

_____

_____

_____

## Working with God's Word

*Fill in the blanks.*

1. Jesus passed through _____.

2. A man named Zacchaeus was a chief _____

_____

3. Zacchaeus showed that he was sorry for his sins by returning _____ times as much as he had gotten dishonestly.

4. Jesus said, "Today _____ has come to this house."

5. Jesus came to save what was _____.

*Draw a line under the word that makes each sentence true.*

1. Zacchaeus was very (old—kind—poor—short).

2. The people (shouted—muttered—rejoiced) when Jesus went into Zacchaeus's home.

3. Zacchaeus offered to give (all—half—most—one-third) of his possessions to the poor.

4. If he had stolen two dollars from a man, he would return (6—2—4—10—8—20) dollars to him.

5. Zacchaeus climbed a (maple—sycamore—pine—apple) tree to see Jesus.

## Applying God's Word

1. How did those who muttered show that they did not understand why Jesus had come to them?

_____

_____

_____

_____

_____

2. In which words did Jesus give the reason for His coming into the world? _____

_____

_____

3. What evidence does this account provide that the Holy Spirit changed the priorities in Zacchaeus's life after Jesus found him? _____

_____

_____

_____

_____

# 74 The Lost Sheep and the Lost Coin
### (Luke 15)

## Thinking about God's Word

1. Who was gathering around to hear Jesus? _____
_____

2. Why do you think Jesus told parables? _____
_____
_____

3. Who is meant by the lost sheep of which Jesus spoke? _____

4. When does a sinner cause joy in heaven? _____
_____

5. What is "the lost" in this parable? _____
_____

## Working with God's Word

*Answer each question correctly with words from the story.*

1. Whom did the teachers and Pharisees mutter about? _____

2. How many sheep were in the flock? _____

3. How many sheep were lost? ___

4. Who went to look for the sheep? _____
_____

5. Who is like the lost sheep? _____

*Draw a line through each sentence that is not true. Write it correctly on the blank line that follows it.*

1. God wants only believers to be saved.
_____

2. Jesus told the parable of the lost sheep.
_____

3. Jesus welcomed sinners and ate with them.
_____

4. A good shepherd would rather lose one sheep than leave 99.
_____

5. There is joy in heaven when a sinner repents.
_____

6. The teachers and Pharisees did not know they were lost sheep.
_____

7. The Son of Man is come to save that which was lost.
_____

## Applying God's Word

1. Who are the "righteous persons who do not need to repent"? _____
_____
_____

2. Were you ever a lost sheep? _____ When?
_____
_____ How did Jesus become your Shepherd? _____
_____

3. How does God's Spirit move the followers of Jesus to show their care and concern for the lost?
_____
_____
_____
_____
_____

# 75 The Lost Son

### (Luke 15)

## Thinking about God's Word

1. What was the "share of the estate" the younger son got from his father? _____
_____

2. What did the younger son do with his inheritance after he received it? _____
_____

3. Find the words the son planned to use to say that he had sinned greatly and no longer deserved his father's love. Which words show that he had become humble? _____
_____
_____
_____

4. How can you tell that he was truly sorry for what he had done? _____
_____

5. How did he confess his sin? _____
_____
_____
How did he admit that he did not deserve forgiveness? _____
_____

6. How did the father show that he had never stopped loving his son and that he had already forgiven him? _____
_____ What did the father show by taking back his son as a member of his family? _____
_____

7. What did the father mean when he said, "For this son of mine was dead and is alive again"? _____
_____
_____
_____

## Working with God's Word

*Answer each question.*
1. Who told this parable? _____
2. How did the son spend his goods? _____
_____
3. Why did the son feed pigs? _____
_____

4. What kind of food would the son gladly have eaten? _____
_____

5. How can you tell that the father had been waiting for his son? _____
_____
_____

6. Of whom is the father of this lesson a true picture? _____

7. Of whom does the prodigal son remind you? ___

*Draw a circle around Yes or No.*
1. Did the younger son ask for his portion of the possessions?  Yes  No

2. Did the prodigal son waste his money?  Yes   No

3. Did the son herd sheep during the famine?
Yes   No

4. Did the prodigal son know that he had sinned?
Yes   No

5. Does knowing that you have sinned bring forgiveness?  Yes  No

6. Did the father meet his son in a far country?
Yes   No

7. Was the prodigal son sorry for his sins?
Yes   No

## Applying God's Word

1. When have you acted like the younger son? _____
_____
_____the older son? _____
_____
_____
_____

2. Did the father like the son's bad deeds? _____
How did he show that he loved him just the same? _____
_____ How did the father's never-ending love help the son? _____
_____
_____

3. Does God love the sins we do? _____ What can this parable mean to our lives? _____
_____
_____

# 76 The Foolish Rich Man
## (Luke 12)

## Thinking about God's Word

1. What is an abundance of possessions? _____
_____

2. What did the rich man want to do? _____
_____
_____

3. What does "eat, drink and be merry" mean?
_____
_____

4. What was going to happen to the rich man? ____
_____

5. What does Jesus say will happen to people who seek His kingdom? _____
_____

## Working with God's Word

*Answer each question.*

1. What did Jesus tell His disciples to be on guard against? _____

2. What produced a good crop for the rich man?
_____

3. What did the rich man want to do with his grain and goods? _____
_____

4. What did God say would happen to the rich man that night? _____

5. What did Jesus tell His disciples not to worry about? _____
_____

*Cross out the false words. Rewrite the sentences to make them true.*

1. "The Foolish Rich Man" is a proverb.
_____

2. Jesus told this parable to the children.
_____

3. God told the rich man that he would die that weekend.
_____

4. Jesus told His disciples they should worry about their lives.
_____

5. Jesus said that people should seek His kingdom when they want.
_____

## Applying God's Word

1. What was wrong with the priorities of the rich man? _____
_____

2. What does it mean to be "rich toward God"? ____
_____
_____
_____

3. Why do God's people not need to worry? _____
_____
_____
_____
_____

# 77 The Pharisee and the Tax Collector
## (Luke 18)

## Thinking about God's Word

1. How did the Pharisee show that he thought himself righteous when he spoke his prayer? _____ _____ _____

2. How did the Pharisee show in the words of his prayer that he despised others? _____ _____ _____

3. In which words did the Pharisee try to tell God of his good deeds instead of his sins? _____ _____ _____ Why did he not ask for forgiveness of sins? _____ _____

4. In whose wisdom, goodness, and righteousness did the tax collector put his trust? _____

5. What did the tax collector confess himself to be before God? _____

6. How did his actions show that he did not consider himself worthy to come to God? _____ _____

7. What was the only thing he asked of God? _____ _____

## Working with God's Word

*Answer each question.*

1. Which is the only way to heaven? _____ _____

2. How do some people wish to enter heaven? _____ _____

3. To whom did Jesus speak this parable? _____ _____ _____

4. Where did two men go to pray? _____

5. Who were the two men? _____ _____

6. For what did the Pharisee thank God? _____ _____

7. What was the tax collector's prayer? _____ _____

8. Who trusted in himself to gain heaven? _____ _____

9. Who trusted in God's mercy for salvation? _____ _____

*Draw a line under the word or phrase that makes each sentence true.*

1. The Bible tells of (two ways—many ways—one way) that it is possible for us to be saved.

2. We (can—cannot—sometimes can) be saved by our own deeds.

3. (One—Two—Three—Four) men went up to the temple to pray.

4. The (tax collector—Pharisee) thanked God that he was not like others.

5. The Pharisee fasted (once—twice—three times) a week.

6. The tax collector said he was a (Pharisee—child of God—sinner—son of Abraham).

7. The tax collector went down to his house (justified—condemned—lost).

## Applying God's Word

1. To whom did Jesus speak this parable? _____ _____ _____ _____ What did they think of themselves? _____ What did they think of others? _____ _____

2. Read the Pharisee's "prayer" carefully. For what did he ask God? _____

3. What does it mean to be humble before God? _____ _____ How does God exalt the humble? _____ _____ _____ _____

# 78 The Good Samaritan
## (Luke 10)

## Thinking about God's Word

1. What two questions did the expert in the law wish to have answered? _____
_____
_____

2. What happened to the man who was going from Jerusalem to Jericho? _____
_____ Which words tell that the wounded man had only a small chance to live?
_____

3. Who came down that road? _____

4. Which words say that the Levite also passed the dying man without helping him? _____
_____

5. What did Jesus ask the expert in the law at the end of His parable? _____
_____
_____
_____

6. How did the expert in the law himself now answer the question he had asked Jesus? _____
_____

7. How did Jesus tell him to be a neighbor? _____
_____

## Working with God's Word

*Fill in the blanks.*

1. Jesus told this parable to an _____
_____.

2. A man went down from Jerusalem to _____.

3. Robbers _____ his clothes.

4. A priest passed by on the _____ side when he saw him.

5. A _____ also looked on him and passed by.

6. A Samaritan had _____ on him.

7. He poured oil and _____ into his wounds.

8. He brought the wounded man to an _____.

9. The Samaritan said to the host, "_____ after him."

10. Jesus said to the expert in the law, "Go and do _____."

*If a sentence is true, mark it T; if false, mark it F.*

1. ___ While going to Jerusalem, a man fell into the hands of robbers.

2. ___ The man was stripped of his clothes and was left half dead.

3. ___ The priest and the Levite were true friends in need.

4. ___ The wounded man was the Good Samaritan.

5. ___ Jesus told this parable to teach the meaning of being a neighbor.

6. ___ A person who loves God truly will love his or her neighbor too.

## Applying God's Word

1. In what ways was the Samaritan a neighbor to the wounded man? _____
_____
_____
_____
_____

2. What did the expert in the law not understand about himself relative to the Law? _____
_____
_____

3. How did Jesus prove Himself to be a good neighbor to us? _____
_____
_____
_____
_____

# 79 The Triumphal Entry
## (Matthew 21)

### Thinking about God's Word

1. Why did Jesus send two disciples ahead to Bethphage? _____
_____ How was He going to use the animals?
_____
_____

2. Horses were used by soldiers and kings for warlike purposes. Donkeys were used in the everyday life of the people for moving people and things from place to place. How did Jesus show that He was coming to Jerusalem for a peaceful purpose?
_____
_____

3. Which prophecy was fulfilled when Jesus entered Jerusalem? _____
_____
_____

What here is meant by the "Daughter of Zion"?
_____
_____

Who was the King who came to her? _____

4. What did the crowd do to honor Jesus as their King? _____
_____
_____

5. What did the people shout? _____
_____
_____
_____

### Working with God's Word

*Fill the blanks with the correct words.*

1. The disciples went to a city on the Mount of _____.

2. Only _____ of Jesus' disciples were sent to find the donkey.

3. The disciples found the donkey in the city of _____.

4. The disciples placed their _____ on the donkey as a saddle.

5. The people cried, "_____ to the Son of David!"

6. Some honored Jesus by _____ tree branches on the road.

7. Others spread their _____ on the road.

*Draw a line under the correct answer to each question.*

1. Toward which city were Jesus and His disciples going? (Capernaum—Bethlehem—Jerusalem—Jericho)

2. Which sad part of Jesus' life was soon to begin? (flight—preaching—suffering—ascension)

3. Which animal was found tied with the donkey? (colt—horse—sheep—watch dog)

4. Who spoke the words, "Say to the Daughter of Zion"? (the Lord—Moses—a prophet—the disciples)

5. Who rode on the donkey? (Jesus—the Daughter of Zion—the disciples)

6. What name did the multitude give to Jesus? (Hosanna—Son of David—Rabbi—Savior)

7. What did Jesus show Himself to be in this lesson? (King—Savior—mighty—rich—kind)

### Applying God's Word

1. Explain the meaning of the designation "Son of David." _____
_____
_____
_____

2. How did Jesus' words to His disciples show Him to be true God? _____
_____
_____

3. Explain Jesus' purpose in going to Jerusalem.
_____
_____

# 80 The Anointing
### (Mark 14; John 12)

## Thinking about God's Word

1. In what city did the anointing take place?
_____

2. Who served at the dinner for Jesus?
_____

3. Who was reclining at the table with Jesus?
_____

4. What did Mary do with the perfume? _____
_____

5. Why did the people there rebuke Mary? _____
_____
_____

6. Why did Jesus tell them to leave her alone? _____
_____
_____

7. What did Jesus say would be done in memory of Mary? _____
_____
_____
_____

## Working with God's Word

*Fill in the blanks with a word from below.*

1. Jesus arrived in Bethany _____ days before Passover.
2. A _____ was given in Jesus' honor.
3. Mary poured _____ on Jesus' feet.
4. She wiped His feet with her _____.

5. Some said, "Why this _____ of perfume?"
6. Jesus said, "The poor you will _____ have with you."
7. The perfume was to prepare for Jesus' _____.
8. _____ betrayed Jesus.

| | | | |
|---|---|---|---|
| dinner | use | always | hair |
| Judas | six | five | perfume |
| waste | burial | | |

## Applying God's Word

1. How did Martha and Mary differ in the way they honored Jesus at the dinner? _____
_____
_____
_____

2. Some well-intentioned believers may have been among those who criticized Mary's action. Explain. _____
_____
_____
_____

3. Compare Mary's actions toward Jesus with those of Judas. _____
_____
_____
_____

## Recalling God's Word

*Match the following by drawing lines.*

1. Jesus went to
2. A dinner was given
3. Martha
4. Mary
5. The perfume was
6. Jesus' feet were wiped with
7. Judas

a. in Jesus' honor.
b. anointed Jesus' feet.
c. hair.
d. expensive.
e. Bethany.
f. went to betray Jesus.
g. served at the table.

# 81 The Last Judgment
### (Matthew 25)

## Thinking about God's Word

1. Will this world ever come to an end? _____

   _____

   According to this parable, who will sit on the throne of the kingdom of glory when the world comes to an end? _____
   _____

2. Who will be gathered before Him? _____
   _____

3. In which words will the righteous say that their righteousness is undeserved and not their own?
   _____
   _____
   _____
   _____
   _____
   _____
   _____

4. Find the words in which the King, Jesus, says that when Christians, in faith, do good works, He counts the deeds as though they had been done to Him. _____
   _____
   _____
   _____

5. Whom will the King condemn into eternal fire?
   _____ In Jesus' own words, why do they deserve this punishment? _____
   _____
   _____
   _____
   _____
   _____
   _____

6. In which words will the cursed say that the punishment is unfair? _____
   _____
   _____
   _____

7. How does the King tell those who are condemned that their own disobedience earned this punishment? _____
   _____
   _____
   _____

8. Where will the wicked then go? _____
   _____
   _____

9. Where will the righteous be taken? _____
   _____
   _____

## Working with God's Word

*Answer each question on the blank line.*

1. Who shall come with the Son of Man on Judgment Day? _____

2. To whom shall the King first speak? _____
   _____

3. Of which kindnesses will the King speak to all before Him? _____
   _____
   _____

4. To whom will the King say, "Depart from Me, you who are cursed"? _____

5. Why will some be condemned to eternal fire?
   _____

*Fill in the blanks of the following sentence with words from below.*

1. When the Son of Man comes on Judgment Day, all the holy _____ shall come with Him.

2. All the _____ will be gathered before Him.

3. First, the King shall speak to those at His _____ hand.

4. Whatever they have done to the least of His _____, they have done to Him.

5. Afterward, the King shall speak to those on His _____ hand.

6. They must depart into eternal _____.

7. The _____ and his angels will be with the wicked.

93

8. Those on the left will go into _____ punishment.

9. But the righteous will go into _____ eternal.

| | | |
|---|---|---|
| right | brothers | nations |
| left | eternal | life |
| devil | angels | priests |
| fire | | |

## Applying God's Word

1. To whom will Jesus give the Kingdom? _____
_____ Why do they
deserve to inherit the Kingdom? _____
_____
_____
_____

2. Who are Jesus' brothers? _____
_____

3. How do we know from this parable that Jesus' followers do not do good works for the purpose of
earning heaven? _____
_____
_____
_____

# 82 The Lord's Supper

**(Luke 22)**

## Thinking about God's Word

1. Which great Jewish festival was drawing near at this time? _____

2. What were some of the preparations necessary according to Exodus 12:3–6? _____
   _____
   _____
   _____
   _____
   _____
   _____
   _____
   _____
   _____
   _____
   _____
   _____
   _____
   _____

3. Whom did Jesus send to prepare the Passover? _____

4. How did Jesus tell His disciples that this would be the last Passover? _____
   _____
   _____

5. Which words show that Judas had become unfaithful before he went to the chief priests? _____

6. As they were eating, what did Jesus give to His disciples? _____
   What did He tell them to do with it? _____
   _____
   What did He say it was? _____
   _____ For whom did Jesus say it was given? _____ In whose memory were they to take it and eat it? _____
   _____

7. What did Jesus tell the disciples to do with the wine that was in the cup? _____

## Working with God's Word

*On the blank lines tell of whom the following things are true.*

1. Who told the disciples that the Son of Man would be crucified? _____

2. Who entered Judas Iscariot? _____

3. Who went to the chief priests to betray Jesus? _____

4. Who went with Peter to prepare the Passover? _____

5. Who sat down with Jesus for the Passover meal? _____

6. Who said, "Take and eat; this is My body"? _____

7. Who said, "What are you willing to give me if I hand Him over to you?" _____

*Draw a line under the words that make the following sentences true.*

1. The chief priests promised to give Judas (10 shekels of silver—gold—30 silver coins—great riches).

2. At the meal there were (10—11—12—13—9—15) people in all.

3. Jesus said that He desired to eat this Passover with the disciples before He (ascended—did more miracles—suffered—went to Galilee).

4. In the Lord's Supper Jesus gives us (bread and wine only—His true body and blood only—His body and blood with the bread and wine).

5. We partake of the Lord's Supper to remind us of (Jesus' birth—the children of Israel in the wilderness—Jesus' first miracle at Cana—Jesus' suffering and death).

## Applying God's Word

1. Jesus broke the bread and gave it to His disciples. When was Jesus' body broken for us? _____

   _____

   _____

   _____

2. Why was Passover a fitting time for Jesus to die for the sins of the world? _____

   _____

   _____

   _____

   _____

   _____

   _____

3. For what purpose did Jesus pour out His blood? _____ Why should God's people receive the Lord's Supper often?

   _____

   _____

   _____

   _____

   _____

# 83 Jesus in Gethsemane
## (Matthew 26; Luke 22)

## Thinking about God's Word

1. Who led the way to the Mount of Olives? _____

2. How did Jesus warn His disciples about what they would all do that night? _____
_____
_____

3. Which words describe the change that the disciples saw coming over Jesus? _____
_____ Which words of Jesus describe His great sorrow? _____
_____
_____

4. Whom did Jesus take with Him to Gethsemane? _____

5. What was the "cup" of which Jesus spoke to His Father? _____

6. How often did Jesus go to pray alone? _____
_____ With which words did He declare that He wanted God's will to be done? _____

7. How many times did Jesus come to the three disciples who were to watch with Him? _____
_____ What did He find them doing each time? _____ With which words did He admonish them the first time? _____
_____
_____
_____
_____

## Working with God's Word

*Answer each question correctly with one word or a short phrase.*

1. Who said that he would never fall away from Jesus? _____

2. How often would Peter disown Jesus that night? _____

3. What did Jesus ask the heavenly Father to take from Him? _____

4. Which part of each disciple was very willing to help Jesus? _____

5. Which part of each disciple was weak? _____

6. Who came from heaven to strengthen Jesus? _____

7. As what were the great drops of sweat that fell to the ground? _____

*If a sentence is true, write T; if it is false, write F.*

1. ___ Jesus said that all the disciples would fall away that night.

2. ___ Peter trusted in himself not to disown Jesus.

3. ___ Jesus said that Peter would disown Him before the rooster would crow.

4. ___ Three disciples went into Gethsemane with Jesus.

5. ___ Simon Peter watched with Jesus in Gethsemane.

6. ___ Jesus prayed three times in the garden.

7. ___ While Jesus suffered greatly, the three disciples slept.

## Applying God's Word

1. Where did Jesus go for strength as He anticipated His coming suffering? _____
_____
_____

2. What did Jesus ask His disciples to pray about? _____
_____
_____

3. How did Jesus indicate His unwavering faithfulness to serve and obey His heavenly Father? _____
_____

# 84 Jesus Is Betrayed and Arrested
## (Matthew 26; John 18)

## Thinking about God's Word

1. Who came with Judas to help in capturing Jesus? _____ _____

2. By which words did Jesus freely give Himself up to the mob? _____

3. How did Judas prove himself a hypocrite when he greeted and kissed Jesus? _____ _____

4. How did Jesus point out to Peter that there was a way of getting help from His Father if it were needed or wished for? _____ _____ _____

## Working with God's Word

*On the blank lines tell of whom the following things are true.*

1. He said, "Who is it you want?" _____

2. They said, "Jesus of Nazareth." _____

3. His ear was cut off. _____ _____

4. He could send more than 72,000 angels to help Jesus. _____

5. They deserted Jesus and fled. _____ _____

## Applying God's Word

1. How did Peter try to save the situation? _____ _____ _____ _____ Why was this foolish as well as wrong? _____ _____ By which words did Jesus teach that "the sword" (earthly force and power) has no place in God's plan for saving people from sin? _____ _____

2. How did Jesus show Himself to be true God in this account? _____ _____

3. Explain how Jesus showed His concern for His disciples even as He was being arrested? _____ _____ _____

## Recalling God's Word

*Match the following by drawing lines to join the parts that make a true sentence.*

1. Judas came

2. Jesus said to them,

3. They drew back

4. Judas said,

5. The Savior said to Judas,

6. The men seized Jesus

7. The high priest's servant

a. and arrested Him.

b. alone.

c. denied Jesus and fled.

d. with a crowd of people.

e. "Greetings, Rabbi!"

f. "Depart from Me!"

g. "Who is it you want?"

h. touched his ear and healed him.

i. and fell to the ground.

j. and worshiped Him.

k. "Are you betraying the Son of Man with a kiss?"

l. had a sword.

m. had his right ear cut off.

## 85 Jesus before the Sanhedrin
### (Matthew 26; John 18)

### Thinking about God's Word

1. Which words indicate that the chief priests, the elders, and the council didn't want to give Jesus a fair trial but had made up their minds to put Him to death even before they had questioned Him?

   _____
   _____
   _____
   _____ Why did
   Jesus' trial *have* to be an unfair one? _____
   _____

2. In which words did Caiaphas ask Jesus if He was the promised Messiah? _____

   _____
   What did Jesus answer? _____
   _____

3. What was the sin of blasphemy of which Jesus was said to be guilty? _____
   _____ Was He guilty? _____
   _____

### Working with God's Word

*Answer each question on the blank line.*

1. Who was Caiaphas? _____
2. Who were assembled with Caiaphas? _____

   _____
3. About which things did the high priest ask Jesus?

   _____
4. Who struck Jesus? _____
5. Why did the Sanhedrin seek evidence against Jesus? _____
6. What did Caiaphas tell Jesus to tell him under oath by the living God? _____

   _____
7. What did the high priest say of Jesus' answer?

   _____
8. With which words did all the men of the Sanhedrin condemn Jesus? _____

   _____
9. In which words did the soldiers mock Jesus after blindfolding Him? _____

   _____

*Draw a line under the correct answer to each question.*

1. To whom was Jesus led by the crowd?
   (Peter—Pontius Pilate—Caiaphas—Nicodemus)

2. Concerning what did the high priest ask Jesus?
   (hands and feet—disciples and teaching—mother and brethren)

3. To whom had Jesus spoken openly?
   (the world—believers only—all except Jews)

4. Who asked Jesus to take an oath?
   (a Roman officer—the high priest—Annas—Pontius Pilate)

5. Did Jesus ever take an oath?
   (no—yes—the Bible doesn't tell—every day)

6. Why was Jesus condemned to death by the Sanhedrin?
   (He had not obeyed Caesar—He called Himself Christ—He would not answer)

7. How did the men who held Jesus speak of Him?
   (very highly—they said only good things—blasphemously—kindly)

### Applying God's Word

1. From what you yourself have learned of Jesus' life, cite with five or six phrases actions that indicate Jesus was the Christ, the Son of God.

   _____
   _____
   _____
   _____
   _____

2. Why didn't Caiaphas believe Jesus when He said, "It is as you say"? _____

   _____
   _____

3. The Sanhedrin said of Jesus, "He is worthy of death." In what sense were their words inappropriate? _____
   _____ In what sense were these
   words true and appropriate? _____

   _____
   _____

# 86 Peter Disowns Jesus; Judas Dies

(Matthew 26–27; Luke 22; John 18)

## Thinking about God's Word

1. To deny means that a person does not want to admit or confess something. What did Peter first deny? _____
Why was that a sin? _____
_____
_____
_____

2. To deny a person means to disown him or not want to know him. In which words did Peter deny Jesus? _____
_____ Why was that a sin?
_____
_____

3. What was the third denial? _____
_____ What sins did Peter add to that of denial? _____
_____

4. How did Jesus call Peter to repentance? _____
_____ Which words describe Peter's great sorrow over his sin?
_____
_____
_____
_____
_____

5. Which words speak of the sorrow that Judas felt when he saw that Jesus was condemned? _____
_____
_____
_____
_____

6. What did the priests say to Judas? _____
_____

7. How did Judas let unbelief rob him of life? _____
_____

## Working with God's Word

*Fill in the blanks correctly.*

1. Peter stood with the servants and officers to see the _____.

2. The _____ who kept the door said Peter was a disciple.

3. Peter _____ that he was a disciple.

4. Peter denied _____ times.

5. Judas repented and brought the ____ silver coins to the priests.

6. Judas said he had betrayed _____ blood.

7. Finally, Judas went and _____ himself.

*Draw a line under the correct answer to each question.*

1. To which place had Peter followed Jesus? (Galilee—temple—Herod's palace—high priest's palace)

2. How many times did Peter deny that he knew Jesus? (1—2—3)

3. How could it be known that Peter was from Galilee? (by his clothing—by his accent—by his face—by his age)

4. How was Peter reminded of Jesus' warning? (by a word—by a look—by a girl—by a sword)

5. How did Peter show his repentance? (he wept—he went to the priests—he left Jesus—he went home)

6. How did Judas show sorrow for his sin? (he cried—he went to Jesus—he gave back the silver—he bought a field)

7. With what sin did all the sins of Judas end? (adultery—coveting—cursing—suicide—swearing)

## Applying God's Word

1. Explain the difference between the sorrow of Peter and the sorrow of Judas. _____
_____
_____
_____
_____

2. What evidence can you cite from this account that one sin leads to another? _____
_____
_____
_____

3. How do God's people today deny Jesus as their Savior? _____
_____
_____
_____
_____

**Jesus before Pilate**

**(Matthew 27; John 18)**

## Thinking about God's Word

1. What charges did the Sanhedrin bring against Jesus? _____ _____ _____ Why was this a serious charge before the Roman governor? _____ _____ _____ _____

2. By which words did Jesus make Pilate curious about His kingdom? _____ _____ How did Jesus answer the question as to whether He is a king? _____ _____ _____ _____ _____

3. In which words did Jesus tell Pilate why He had come into the world? _____ _____ _____ _____ _____

4. In which words did Pilate declare Jesus guiltless? _____ _____ How did he in the same breath treat Jesus as one who deserved punishment? _____ _____ _____ Was that just? _____ Why? _____ _____ _____

5. How did the people show that they wanted Jesus to be put to death? _____ _____

6. What unfair treatment did Pilate let the soldiers give Jesus even when he knew that Jesus was without fault? _____ _____ _____

7. How did the chief priests and officers show only blind hatred in their hearts for Jesus? _____ _____

## Working with God's Word

*Answer each question with Yes or No.*

1. Did the Sanhedrin deliver Jesus to Caiaphas, the governor? ____

2. Did the Sanhedrin call Jesus guilty because He had been subverting the nation? ____

3. Did Pilate ask Jesus, "Are You the king of the Jews?" ____

4. Did Pilate say, "I have found many faults in this man"? ____

5. Did Pilate want to release Jesus? ____

6. Did the priests, rulers, and people want to release Jesus? ____

7. Did Pilate have Jesus flogged? ____

8. Did the people want Pilate to crucify Jesus? ____

*Draw a line under the words that make each sentence true.*

1. Pilate was the (high priest—governor—king).

2. The people accused Jesus of calling Himself (Caesar—God—a king—Governor).

3. Pilate asked Jesus if He were a (God—king—Christian—Roman).

4. Jesus (was—wasn't) a king.

5. Pilate soon found out that Jesus (was guilty—was true God—was innocent—was the Savior of the world).

6. The crown that Jesus wore was made of (thorns—gold—purple—reeds).

7. When Pilate brought Jesus forth, he said, ("Crucify Him!"—"Flog Him!"—"Here is the man!"—"Scourge Him!")

8. Pilate washed his hands to show that (Jesus was innocent—he was innocent—the Jews were innocent).

9. At last Pilate said that Jesus should be (put into prison—crucified—set free—sent to Rome).

## Applying God's Word

1. How does Jesus' kingship differ from that which Pilate had in mind as he questioned Jesus?

_____

_____

_____

_____

_____

2. Since Pilate declared Jesus to be innocent, why did he not set Him free? _____

_____ How did he try to "wash his hands" of Jesus' blood? _____

_____

_____

_____

_____ Who asked that the punishment for this day's evil deeds come upon them?

_____ Actually, who paid for the sins of Pilate and Jesus' accusers? _____

_____

3. Explain how and why Jesus suffered under Pontius Pilate. _____

_____

_____

_____

_____

_____

_____

# 88 Jesus Is Crucified
## (Luke 23; John 19)

## Thinking about God's Word

1. How did the soldiers carry out the will of the Jewish leaders by order of the governor? _____ _____

2. How do we know that even in His great agony Jesus thought of the welfare of His mother? _____ _____ Who was to take care of her from now on? _____

3. Which prayer to Jesus shows that one of the criminals repented in his dying hour? _____ _____ _____ What certain promise did Jesus give him? _____ _____ _____

## Working with God's Word

*Fill in the blanks.*

1. Jesus carried His own _____ when He went to be crucified.

2. He went to a place called _____.

3. Two _____ were crucified with Jesus.

4. One criminal said, "Aren't You the _____? Save Yourself and us!"

5. Darkness came over the land at the _____ hour.

*Circle Yes or No.*

1. A soldier carried Jesus' body.   Yes   No

2. Jesus asked God to bring revenge upon His enemies.   Yes   No

3. Two criminals were crucified with Jesus. Yes   No

4. The darkness over the land began at the third hour.   Yes   No

5. Jesus asked Peter to care for His mother, Mary. Yes   No

## Applying God's Word

1. With which prayer did Jesus ask forgiveness for those who had brought Him to His death? _____ _____

   In what way does this prayer also include you? _____ _____

2. What did Jesus cry out at the ninth hour? _____ _____ _____ Which words show that this may have been the time of His greatest suffering? _____ Because of whose sins had God forsaken Him? _____

3. What knowledge did one of the criminals on the cross have of the Christ? _____ _____ _____ _____ _____

   What knowledge did he lack? _____ _____ _____ _____

# 89 Jesus Dies and Is Buried
## (Matthew 27; Luke 23; John 19)

## Thinking about God's Word

1. What was Jesus given to drink? _____

2. What did Jesus say after He drank? _____
_____

3. What did Jesus say before He died? _____
_____

4. How did one member of the council show honor to Jesus' body? _____
How did another man show his love for Jesus openly? _____
_____

5. How did the very fact that they were anointing Jesus show that these friends had not understood what Jesus had spoken of in Luke 18:31–34?
_____
_____
_____
_____

6. After burying His body, how did the friends of Jesus make His grave secure? _____
_____
_____ How did God use the enemies of Jesus to make the grave still more secure?
_____
_____
_____

7. The chief priests and Pharisees did not believe Jesus would rise. Why then did they want His grave guarded? _____
_____
_____
_____

## Working with God's Word

*Answer the questions correctly on the blank lines.*

1. Why did the Jewish leaders want the legs of those who had been crucified broken? _____
_____

2. Why were Jesus' legs not broken? _____
_____

3. How did the soldiers make sure that Jesus was dead? _____
_____

4. Which women saw where Jesus was laid? _____
_____
_____

5. What did the women do on the Sabbath Day?
_____

6. Who met with Pilate the next day? _____
_____

7. How did Jesus' enemies make the tomb secure?
_____
_____
_____

*Write T if the sentence is true; write F if the sentence is false.*

1. ____ Nicodemus asked that the legs of the crucified men be broken.

2. ____ The soldiers broke the two criminals' legs.

3. ____ Jesus' legs were pierced with a spear.

4. ____ Joseph of Arimathea was a follower of Jesus.

5. ____ Nicodemus brought a mixture of myrrh and aloes.

6. ____ Jesus' 11 disciples buried Him.

7. ____ The friends of Jesus rested on the Sabbath Day.

8. ____ Jesus' enemies knew that He had said, "After three days I will rise again."

9. ____ Pilate gave the disciples a guard.

10. ____ Jesus' disciples sealed the stone.

## Applying God's Word

1. Why were Jesus' legs not broken? See Numbers 9:12. _____
_____

2. How did the piercing of Jesus' side fulfill a prophecy of the Old Testament? See Zechariah 12:10. _____
_____

3. What did Jesus accomplish for us through His death? _____
_____
_____

# 90 The Resurrection of Christ

## (Matthew 28; Mark 16)

## Thinking about God's Word

1. On what day had Jesus died? _____ During which full day was He dead? _____ How can you tell that it was now the third day? _____
_____
_____

2. Why did the women go to the tomb? _____
_____ What question did they ask on the way? _____
_____
_____

3. Who had already rolled the stone away? _____
_____ Who became alarmed when they saw him? _____

4. To whom did Mary Magdalene run when she saw that the stone was rolled away? _____
_____
_____ What did she think? _____
_____

5. With what glorious message did the angel explain the empty grave? _____

6. To whom were the women to tell the glad news first? _____ Whose name was especially mentioned? _____

7. Where would the disciples see Jesus with their own eyes? _____

## Working with God's Word

*Answer each question with one or two words.*

1. Of whom is it said that they shook and became like dead men? _____

2. Who said, "They have taken the Lord out of the tomb"? _____

3. Who was the disciple whom Jesus loved? _____

4. Who said, "He has risen! He is not here"?
_____

5. Who entered the tomb and saw a young man?
_____

*Answer each question by circling Yes or No.*

1. Did the women go to the grave on the Sabbath Day? Yes No

2. Is Sunday the first day of the week? Yes No

3. Did the angel roll the stone away to let Jesus out? Yes No

4. Did Salome tell Peter and John that the tomb was empty? Yes No

5. Did all the women enter Jesus' tomb? Yes No

6. Was an angel in the tomb? Yes No

7. Did Jesus arise from the dead on Sunday? Yes No

8. Did the disciples steal Jesus' body? Yes No

9. Was Jesus in the grave until the third day? Yes No

10. Did Jesus break the chains of death for us? Yes No

## Applying God's Word

1. How do you know the women did not expect Jesus to rise from the dead? _____
_____
_____
_____

2. Why were the women afraid, yet joyful, as they left the empty tomb? _____
_____
_____
_____

3. Read the entire message of the angel. Note how many things he said in those few words. What are they? _____
_____
_____
_____
_____
_____
_____ Which is the most important to you? _____
_____
_____

# 91 The First Appearances of the Risen Lord
## (Matthew 28; John 20)

## Thinking about God's Word

1. Who were the first people to whom the risen Lord appeared? _____

2. Why did Mary not recognize Jesus at first? _____ _____ What did she say when Jesus said her name? _____ _____

3. What message did Jesus tell her to give the disciples? _____ _____ _____

4. What did Jesus call the disciples? _____ _____ What did this show about His love for them, even though they had forsaken Him three days ago? _____ _____ _____

5. How did the words *go* and *tell* show that Jesus was thinking of others who were fearful and needed comfort? _____ _____ _____

## Working with God's Word

*Each sentence below has one mistake in it. Draw a line through the wrong word and write the correct one in its place.*

1. Mary stood near the tomb, sleeping. _____ _____

2. Peter asked her whom she was seeking. _____ _____

3. Mary thought that Jesus was an angel. _____ _____

4. Rabboni means "Messiah." _____ _____

5. Mary Magdalene told the women that she had seen the Lord. _____

6. Jesus met the women and said to them, "All glory!" _____

7. They held Jesus by the feet, and they kissed Him. _____

8. The guards told the chief officers all the things that had happened. _____

9. The soldiers were paid to say, "His enemies came during the night and stole Him away." _____ _____

*Draw a line under the words that make each sentence true.*

1. Jesus said to her, ("Greetings!"—"Rabboni"—"Mary"—"Don't cry").

2. Mary said to Jesus, ("Greetings"—"Rabboni"—"Mary"—"Don't cry").

3. Mary Magdalene told (Jesus' mother—the disciples—the women—the chief priests) that she had seen Jesus.

4. The (disciples—guards—women—Pharisees) told the chief priests what had been done at the grave.

5. The soldiers were given (promises—punishment—money) to lie.

## Applying God's Word

1. Why was Mary not with the other women to hear the angel's message? _____ _____ _____

2. How did the women respond when they met the resurrected Christ? _____ _____

3. Mary didn't recognize the risen Jesus until Jesus spoke to her. How does Jesus speak to people today to bring them to recognize Himself as their Lord and Savior? _____ _____ _____

# 92 Christ Appears to His Disciples

## (John 20; Matthew 28)

### Thinking about God's Word

1. When did Jesus appear to His disciples? _____
_____ What was the disciples'
reaction? _____
_____
_____

2. With which words did Jesus greet the disciples?
_____

3. How did Jesus now let the doubting disciples con-
vince themselves that He was really the same
Jesus who had lived among them before His
death? _____
_____ Read the words that show that
the disciples now believed. _____
_____
_____

4. As the risen Lord who would live forever, Jesus
gave His servants a last command. What are the
words of this important commission? _____
_____
_____
_____
_____
_____
_____
_____
_____
_____

5. From the Great Commission, write the words
that tell

a. that the One giving the command is the Lord
of heaven and earth; _____
_____
_____

b. that the disciples were to go to others instead
of waiting for them to come to them; _____
_____

c. who was to go; _____

d. what they were to do; _____
_____
_____
_____
_____
_____

e. whom they were to teach and baptize; _____
_____

f. in whose name they were to baptize; _____
_____
_____

g. what things they should teach. _____
_____

### Working with God's Word

*Fill in the blanks.*

1. The doors were _____ for fear of the Jews.

2. Jesus said unto them, "Why are you
_____?"

3. He _____ them His hands and His feet.

4. The _____ were overjoyed when they
saw the Lord.

5. Jesus _____ on His disciples.

6. Then the 11 _____ went into Galilee.

7. There they worshiped Him, but some
_____.

8. Jesus said, "Go and make disciples of all
_____."

9. Jesus said, "I am with you _____."

*Fill in the blanks with words from below.*

1. Jesus came to His disciples on the _____ day of the week.

2. Jesus stood among them and said, " _____ be with you."

3. The disciples thought that they saw a _____.

4. Jesus said, "A ghost does not have _____ _____."

5. Jesus said, "If you forgive anyone his _____, they are forgiven."

| | | |
|---|---|---|
| first | body and blood | flesh and bones |
| peace | ghost | second |
| sins | nations | |

## Applying God's Word

1. By what sign did Jesus show that He was now giving them the Holy Spirit? _____ _____ What important power did He give them? _____ _____

2. With which words did Jesus now remind them that He was no longer the humble Servant, but the exalted Lord of heaven and earth? _____ _____ _____

3. What tasks did Jesus give His disciples after His resurrection? _____ _____ _____ _____ _____ _____ _____

# 93 The Ascension

## (Acts 1)

## Thinking about God's Word

1. In which words did Jesus promise a special gift to His disciples? _____ _____ Where were they to wait until He sent it? _____ Which words tell what the gift would be? _____ _____

2. Where did Jesus lead His disciples after He had spoken to them? _____ Why did He lift up His hands? _____ _____

3. How did God's messengers announce that Jesus will come again? _____ _____ _____ _____

4. How do you know the disciples understood the words of the angels? _____ _____ _____

## Working with God's Word

*Answer each question Yes or No.*

1. Is Jesus' resurrection absolutely true? ____
2. Did Jesus say, "Wait for the gift My Father promised"? ____
3. Did John baptize with water? ____
4. Did Jesus ask the disciples to stay in Bethany? ____
5. Did Jesus and His disciples go to Bethany? ____
6. Did Jesus bless His disciples before He left them? ____
7. Were two men standing by the disciples as Jesus ascended? ____
8. Will Jesus come again in the same way as He ascended? ____
9. Did the disciples worship the angels before returning? ____

*Cross out the sentences that are not true. Write them correctly on the blanks.*

1. Jesus lived on earth 40 years after His resurrection.

_____

2. The disciples were to leave Jerusalem and start preaching immediately.

_____

3. Jesus ascended into heaven at Bethany.

_____

4. Twelve disciples saw Jesus ascend.

_____

5. An angel stood by the disciples as Jesus ascended.

_____

6. Jesus now sits at the right hand of God.

7. We will see Jesus someday.

_____

8. The disciples were sad when they returned to Jerusalem.

_____

## Applying God's Word

1. Why did Jesus show Himself on earth after He had proven His power over death and the devil?

_____

2. In what way was Jesus no longer to be with His disciples? _____ In what way would He remain with them all the time? _____ _____ _____

3. How did the disciples respond after Jesus' ascension? _____ How are Jesus' disciples still responding in the same way today? _____ _____ _____

# 94  The Holy Spirit Comes at Pentecost
### (Acts 2)

## Thinking about God's Word

1. What signs indicated the Holy Spirit entered the room in which the disciples were gathered? _____ _____ _____ _____ _____ What showed that the Spirit had entered the disciples? _____ _____

2. By what miracle did the disciples show that the Holy Spirit had come upon them? _____ _____ _____ Which words tell that the Holy Spirit told them what to say? _____

3. Which words of the people give us an idea of what things the disciples preached? _____ _____

4. What did some in the crowd say of this Pentecost miracle? _____ _____ Why? _____ _____ _____ _____

5. Tell how Peter began the work of "catching men" that Jesus had foretold in Matthew 4:18–19. _____ _____

6. Read Peter's words. According to Peter, what did Jesus' miracles, His suffering and death, and His resurrection prove Him to be? _____ _____ Why could Peter be so sure of Jesus' power to do miracles, of His death, and of His resurrection? _____ _____

7. How can you tell that Peter was now filled with the Holy Spirit? _____ _____ _____ _____ _____

## Working with God's Word

*On the blank lines tell of whom the following things are true.*

1. He gave the disciples power to speak in other tongues. _____

2. God-fearing people were there from every nation under heaven. _____

3. They were all amazed and bewildered. _____ _____

4. They said, "They have had too much wine." _____ _____

5. He said, "Men of Israel, listen to this." _____

6. He told the people to repent and to be baptized. _____

7. People must repent and be baptized in His name. _____

*Draw a line under the words that make each sentence true.*

1. The disciples began to speak in other (voices—fires—tongues).

2. (The Holy Spirit—The Son—The Father) came upon the disciples.

3. Jesus had been accredited by God by (the Jews—everyone—miracles).

4. (Peter—The Holy Spirit—The disciples) opened the hearts of the people so that they repented.

5. About (30,000—300,000—3,000—300) people became Christians that day.

## Applying God's Word

1. For what purpose was the Spirit's power released at Pentecost? _____

   _____

   _____

   _____

2. Which words show that the people were sorry for what they had done? _____

   _____

   _____

   _____

   _____ How did Peter tell them they could obtain forgiveness for all their sins?

   _____

   _____

   _____

   _____

   _____

   _____

   _____

   How did the Lord bless the words spoken by Peter? _____

   _____

   _____

   _____

3. Who is included among the recipients of God's promise in Christ Jesus? _____

   _____

   _____

# 95 The Crippled Beggar Is Healed
## (Acts 3)

## Thinking about God's Word

1. Why was the crippled man at the gate of the temple? _____
   _____ Why was the temple the best place to which people could be brought if they needed mercy from other people? _____
   _____
   _____

2. What did the lame man expect of Peter and John?
   _____

3. What did the lame man receive that was better than silver and gold? _____

4. How did the man show his thankfulness for what he had received? _____
   _____
   _____
   _____

5. From which words can you see the reason for performing this miracle at the time and in the place it was done? _____
   _____
   _____
   _____
   _____

## Working with God's Word

*Answer each question with one word or a short phrase.*

1. At what time was the crippled man healed?
   _____

2. Who took the crippled man by the hand and helped him up? _____

3. Whom did the crippled man praise? _____

4. Who saw the crippled man walking?
   _____

5. Who spoke to the people? _____

*Draw a line under the words that make each sentence true.*

1. The disciple with Peter was named (Andrew—John—James—Philip).

2. The man could walk again (in the same hour—the next day—immediately—soon afterward).

3. The man was healed by (Peter's—John's —God's—Peter and John's) power.

4. The first place that the healed man went was (to his wife—to Jesus—home—to the temple courts).

5. The people who saw this miracle were brought to Christ by (the miracle—the crippled man—God's Word—the crowd).

6. After Peter's sermon the number of male believers grew to about (3,000—4,000—5,000—10,000).

## Applying God's Word

1. To whom did Peter and John give all glory for the miracles? _____ In which words did Peter tell the people what they had done? _____
   _____ How did he offer the love and forgiveness of Jesus to all?
   _____
   Who were the ones who received forgiveness?
   _____
   _____

2. What words of God's Law did Peter preach?
   _____
   _____
   _____

3. What were Peter's words of Gospel? _____
   _____
   _____
   _____
   What results does God work in people through the Gospel? _____
   _____
   _____

# 96 Stephen

## (Acts 6–8)

### Thinking about God's Word

1. According to Acts 6:1–5, what was Stephen's work? _____ _____ _____

2. Which words tell why Stephen could do miracles? _____ _____

3. Who stirred up the people against Stephen? _____ _____ What accusations did they bring against him? _____ _____ _____

4. Read Stephen's reply to the accusations against him. How had the fathers of the Jews been stiff-necked? _____ _____ Who was the Righteous One who had been betrayed and murdered? _____

5. Which words of the lesson tell that Stephen's words upset his accusers? _____ _____ _____

6. Why could Stephen look into heaven? _____ _____ Whom could he see there? _____ _____

7. Whose name is mentioned as being pleased with Stephen's death? _____

### Working with God's Word

*Fill in the blanks.*

1. Stephen did great _____ _____ among the people.

2. People produced false _____ against Stephen.

3. Stephen said the people were murderers of the _____ One.

4. The men were _____ and gnashed their teeth at him.

5. They rushed at him and _____ him out of the city.

6. Then they _____ Stephen.

7. _____ gave approval to his death.

*Write a T or F in the blank.*

1. ___ Stephen was a man full of God's grace and power.

2. ___ Stephen did great wonders among the people.

3. ___ Those who argued with Stephen found it simple to disprove what he taught.

4. ___ The men who testified against Stephen were honest men.

5. ___ When Stephen spoke to the Sanhedrin, his face shone like the sun.

6. ___ A young man named Saul tried to save Stephen from the hands of the mob.

7. ___ When Stephen died, he asked God to bring revenge upon his murderers.

### Applying God's Word

1. What words of God's Law did Stephen speak? _____ _____ _____ _____ _____ With what result? _____ _____

2. With which simple prayer did Stephen place his soul into the hands of his Lord? _____ _____

3. How did Stephen's last prayer show his enemies that he had a real interest in the salvation of their souls? _____ _____

# 97  Philip and the Ethiopian
## (Acts 8)

## Thinking about God's Word

1. Where did the angel tell Philip to go? _____
_____
_____

2. Whom did Philip meet on the way? _____
_____
_____

3. What did the Spirit tell Philip to do? _____
_____

4. What did Philip ask the man? _____
_____
_____

5. What did Philip do with water? _____
_____

6. What happened to Philip? _____
_____

7. What did the man do? _____
_____

## Working with God's Word

*Fill in the blanks with words from the story.*

1. Philip went south on the road that went from Jerusalem to _____

2. The Ethiopian had gone to _____ to worship.

3. The Ethiopian was reading the Book of _____.

4. He asked _____ to come sit with him.

5. Philip told the Ethiopian the good news about _____.

6. The _____ of the Lord took Philip away.

7. The Ethiopian went on his way _____.

*Put these events in order from 1–7.*

___ Philip baptized the Ethiopian.

___ The Ethiopian was in his chariot reading.

___ Philip sat with the man.

___ Philip met an Ethiopian while he was walking.

___ Philip disappeared.

___ The Ethiopian left rejoicing.

___ Philip explained the good news about Jesus.

## Applying God's Word

1. Explain how the prophecy the Ethiopian read was fulfilled in Jesus. _____
_____
_____
_____

2. How does this account remind us that salvation by grace through faith in Jesus is for all people?
_____
_____
_____

3. Why was the Ethiopian happy? _____
_____

# 98 Saul's Conversion
## (Acts 9)

### Thinking about God's Word

1. How did Saul try to get rid of those who believed Christ's doctrine and taught it to others? _____
_____
_____

2. What happened to Saul on the way to Damascus? _____
_____
_____

3. Whose voice was it that spoke to Saul? _____
What did He say? _____
_____

4. Why did Jesus say that Saul was persecuting Him when he had been persecuting the disciples?
_____
_____

5. Which words show that Saul's heart was changed toward Jesus? _____
_____
_____

6. With which words did Ananias assure Saul that his sins were forgiven? _____
_____
_____
_____ How did
Saul show that he believed the Lord Jesus was His Savior? _____
_____

7. How did Saul now show love instead of hate toward the disciples? _____
_____
_____ Whose name did he preach instead of blaspheme? _____ What did Saul testify of Jesus? _____

### Working with God's Word

*Of whom are the following things true?*

1. He gave Saul letters to the synagogues in Damascus. _____

2. He said, "Saul, Saul, why do you persecute Me?"
_____

3. He said, "Who are You, Lord?" _____

4. He came from Tarsus. _____

5. He lived in Damascus. _____

6. He visited Saul at the Lord's command.
_____

7. He received his sight and was baptized at Damascus. _____

8. They watched the gates of Damascus day and night. _____

9. They lowered Saul in a basket through an opening in the wall. _____

*Draw a line under the word that answers each question correctly.*

1. Where did Saul wish to go to persecute Christians? (Samaria—Tarsus—Jerusalem—Damascus—Capernaum)

2. What did he plan to do with the Christians he found? (kill them—hang them—send them home—take them to Jerusalem)

3. Who spoke to Saul when he fell to the ground? (the soldiers—Jesus—Ananias—the high priest)

4. When he got up, what did Saul find out had happened to him? (He was blind—There was no one—It was night—He closed his eyes)

5. What was the name of the disciple who lived at Damascus? (Judas—Peter—Ananias—Tarsus—John—Andrew)

6. To whom was Saul to bear Jesus' name and His Gospel? (poor people—Samaritans—Gentiles—disciples)

7. When the disciple spoke to Saul, what did he call him? (you sinner—poor sinner—Paul—Brother Saul—sir)

8. How long was Saul in Damascus? (3 weeks—several days—3 days—many years)

9. In whose name did Saul speak when he returned to Jerusalem? (the disciples'—Ananias's—the high priest's—the Lord's)

## Applying God's Word

1. In what way was Saul persecuting Jesus? _____
   _____
   _____
   _____

2. Saul was spiritually blind; then he was given sight.
   Explain. _____
   _____
   _____

3. What happened in Saul's life after he became a
   Christian? _____
   _____
   _____
   _____
   _____

## 99 Peter Is Freed from Prison

(Acts 12)

### Thinking about God's Word

1. Why was King Herod arresting Christians?

   _____

2. Who appeared in the cell? _____

3. What happened to Peter's chains? _____

   _____

4. Where did Peter go? _____

   _____

   _____

5. Who answered the door at Mary's house?

   _____

### Working with God's Word

*Fill in the blanks with words from below.*

King _____ arrested some who belonged to the church. He put _____ in prison. Peter would go on trial after the _____. The members of the _____ were praying for Peter. One night an _____ appeared in Peter's cell. The chains fell off of Peter's _____. Peter followed the _____ out of prison. Then he went to _____ house. The people did not believe it was _____. When they saw him, they were _____.

| | | |
|---|---|---|
| church | angel | Passover |
| Martha's | legs | Peter |
| astonished | Mary's | Herod |
| wrists | | |

*Answer each question.*

1. Where was Peter put? _____

2. What did the angel tell Peter to do? _____

   _____

   _____

   _____

3. What did Peter think he was seeing? _____

4. Why did Peter go to Mary's house? _____

   _____

5. What did the believers in Mary's house think was wrong with the servant girl? _____

   _____

6. What did Peter describe? _____

   _____

### Applying God's Word

1. What does this account reveal to us about the role of angels? _____

   _____

2. Why is the reaction of the people to Peter's release somewhat unexpected? _____

   _____

   _____

3. At the conclusion of the account Peter tells how the Lord rescued him. How might every Christian benefit from Peter's example? _____

   _____

   _____

# 100 Paul's Shipwreck

## (Acts 27–28)

## Thinking about God's Word

1. What was the weather like? _____
2. Why was the cargo thrown overboard? _____
   _____
   _____
3. What did Paul tell the hungry men? _____
   _____
   _____
   _____
   _____
   _____
   _____
4. Who told Paul not to be afraid? _____
5. Where did they decide to run the ship aground?
   _____
6. What were the soldiers going to do with the prisoners? _____
7. How many people died in the shipwreck?
   _____

## Working with God's Word

*Fill in the blanks with words from below.*

1. Paul was sailing to _____.
2. A _____ swept down from the island.
3. The ship took a violent _____ from the storm.
4. Neither sun nor _____ appeared for many days.
5. The men gave up _____ of being saved.
6. An _____ appeared to Paul.
7. The angel said all would be _____.
8. A _____ helped spare Paul's life.
9. The prisoners landed on _____.
10. The islanders were _____.

| | | |
|---|---|---|
| angel | storm | wind |
| Malta | moon | centurion |
| Italy | saved | kind |
| stars | battering | hope |

*Put these events in order from 1 to 7.*

___ Everyone reached land safely.

___ The men gave up hope of being saved.

___ Paul and other prisoners set sail for Italy.

___ The centurion helped Paul stay safe.

___ An angel stood beside Paul.

___ The people of Malta welcomed the men.

___ A wind of hurricane force hit the ship.

## Applying God's Word

1. How did God bless Paul's traveling companions because of Paul? _____
   _____
   _____
2. Paul told the sailors that God would save them. To what message of greater salvation had Paul dedicated his life? _____
   _____
   _____
   _____
3. Tell how this account from Paul's journeys is a metaphor of the Christian life. _____
   _____
   _____
   _____
   _____